LANDMARKS IN LITERATURE

Maynard Mack, *Series Editor*
Yale University

Some books belong to all times and places. They are the rivers, mountains, seas, and continents of our intellectual and moral world. They tell us where we are and how far we have still to go. They are, in short, our landmarks.

Landmarks in Literature is a series of interpretive studies of such books, each written by an authority of today, each a reference point between our present and our past.

DAVID HAYMAN, author of this volume in the Landmarks in Literature series, is Professor of English and Comparative Literature at the University of Iowa. His extensive writings on Joyce include *Joyce et Mallarmé,* a two-volume study in French, *A First-Draft Version of Finnegans Wake,* and major articles in literary journals. Among his articles published in The James Joyce Quarterly are: "From *Finnegans Wake:* A Sentence in Progress"; "Forms of Folly in Joyce: A Study of Clowning in *Ulysses*"; and "Daedalian Imagery in *A Portrait.*"

ULYSSES

THE MECHANICS
OF MEANING

❧ ❧

DAVID HAYMAN

PRENTICE-HALL, INC., ENGLEWOOD CLIFFS, N.J.

Acknowledgment is made to the following publishers for permission to reprint excerpts in this book: From *Finnegans Wake* by James Joyce. Copyright 1939 by James Joyce, renewed 1967 by George Joyce and Lucia Joyce. Reprinted by permission of The Viking Press, Inc. From *A Portrait of the Artist as a Young Man* by James Joyce. Copyright 1916 by B. W. Huebsch, Inc., renewed 1944 by Nora Joyce. Copyright © 1964 by the Estate of James Joyce. All rights reserved. Reprinted by permission of The Viking Press, Inc. From *Ulysses* by James Joyce. Copyright 1914, 1918 by Margaret Caroline Anderson and renewed 1942, 1946 by Nora Joseph Joyce. Reprinted by permission of Random House, Inc. The Joyce schema is reprinted by permission of the Society of Authors as the literary representatives of the James Joyce Estate.

Current printing (last number):
10 9 8 7 6 5 4 3 2 1

PRENTICE-HALL INTERNATIONAL, INC. (*London*)
PRENTICE-HALL OF AUSTRALIA, PTY. LTD. (*Sydney*)
PRENTICE-HALL OF CANADA, LTD. (*Toronto*)
PRENTICE-HALL OF INDIA PRIVATE LIMITED (*New Delhi*)
PRENTICE-HALL OF JAPAN, INC. (*Tokyo*)

❧ PREFACE ❧

A glance at the imposing Joyce bibliography, the acres of words, the conflicting critical positions and varied approaches, the secondary sources and documents, especially such monuments as Richard Ellmann's 800-page biography and the three volumes of letters, will convince anyone that little can be said in a hundred pages about James Joyce's *Ulysses*. But then perhaps we have surrounded the monster with a wall that can still be breached by a modest volume designed to serve the general reader as a descriptive introduction.

There is no room in a book of this sort for a review of critical positions or a rehash of long established "facts" or a careful summary of the action. Instead, I would refer interested readers to some of the books listed in my bibliography. Neither is there room for a full consideration of the relationship of Ireland and Joyce's life to his work or of the function of his theories. The latter have, in my opinion, been taken too seriously by those who would make youthful pronouncements into manifestos and too lightly by those who would have the works spring into being without intellectual bases or literary forebears. For my own part I assume that Joyce's works grow naturally out of literary traditions fostered by the European nineteenth century.

Aiming at the presentation of an integral sense of the novel with an assessment of Joyce's accomplishment and the role of *Ulysses* in his work and in our century, I have deliberately stressed form as it relates to content. It is my conviction that Joyce's contribution is twofold: he has created (1) a most lifelike situation in (2) a most delightful manner. At the risk of seeming mechanical and even pedestrian I have chosen to consider in turn *Ulysses'* action, characters, and setting, the thematic uses of analogy, and the application of paradox, and then the techniques, the structure, and the styles as functional aspects of the book's meaning. Along the way I have stressed certain themes and motifs and attempted to show how through them the book develops the situations of its chief personae. I believe that this approach will suggest the sort of questions one can ask of *Ulysses* and the sort of answers one may expect to get.

I have placed in appendix a copy of the much-reproduced schema for *Ulysses,* a suggestive document which can be used as a partial index to the author's sense of the book but not as a definitive key to its many aspects. Following tradition, I have used Joyce's homeric chapter headings, assuming the presence of analogies discussed in my chapter IV. I have also assumed that the reader will be familiar with both *The Odyssey* and *A Portrait of the Artist as a Young Man.*

❧ CONTENTS ☙

... his usylessly unreadable Blue Book of Eccles, *édition de ténèbres*, (even yet sighs the Most Different, Dr. Poindejenk, authorised bowdler and censor, it can't be repeated!) ...

Finnegans Wake

~§ I §~

BACKGROUNDS

I

James Joyce called *Finnegans Wake* the book of "Doublends Jined."
Ulysses is the book of Dublin. Dublin is conceived to be an anagram
for Ireland, and Ireland to be an aspect of universal history every
detail of which is important (but also impotent) in the general
scheme of the universe created by a God who may have been very
much like "Jeems Joker" himself. But appearances to the contrary,
neither Dublin nor Ireland is a figment of the Joycean imagination.

The Ireland that Leopold Bloom feels is important because he
wishes to belong to it and that Stephen Dedalus values because it
belongs to him was not always the cultural backwater depicted by
Joyce in *Ulysses*, a country praising its own past, a land whose best
and most valuable export is "wild geese" and artists, who fight, each
in his way, on foreign soil. Its history goes back into the night of
prehistory when successive waves of invaders came, conquered, settled, and left their marks even before the Romans invaded and rein-
vaded Britain. Irish recorded history is as turbulent as the shadowy
past of Parthalons, Firbolgs, the fabulous Tuatha Dedannan, and
the sons of Milesius or the Milesians of whom Joyce's citizen-Cyclops
is so proud and whose tales were being rewritten and romanticized
by significant as well as "paltryattic" writers during Joyce's youth.
The annals Joyce used so extensively in *Finnegans Wake* tell of
quarrelsome men, tribal wars, meaningless victories and defeats, invasions, natural disasters or, as Stephen sees it reflected in the play
of small boys at Deasy's school, self-perpetuating carnage:

> Again: a goal. I am among them, among their battling bodies in a
> medley, the joust of life . . . Jousts. Time shocked rebounds, shock
> by shock. Jousts, slush and uproar of battles, the frozen deathspew of
> the slain, a shout of spear spikes baited with men's bloodied guts. (32)[1]

Also buried in prehistory are the Celtic bards and priests or Olavs
of the Druids, children of a highly articulate people which built

1

few permanent monuments but created tales and spells that survived the first historical conquest, Saint Patrick's fifth century spiritual victory in the name of Jesus Christ when, as Joyce comically puts it in *Finnegans Wake*:

> . . . he converted it's nataves . . . through the medium of znigznaks with sotiric zeal, to put off the barcelonas . . . and kiss on their bottes (Master!) as often as they came within bloodshot of that other familiar temple . . .[2]

During the early middle ages Irish monks founded monastic communities amidst warring Irish tribes, or went out as missionaries into a turbulent and barbaric Europe to establish islands of culture. This period, perhaps the greatest of Irish history, was punctuated by the Viking forays of the ninth century, but turning gradually from piracy to trade, the alien Galls built the first permanent cities on the seacoast, towns like Dublin, Galway, Waterford, Wexford, and Cork. A new era came when a handful of Norman knights led by Richard de Clare were invited to settle a quarrel between two Irish chieftains caused by what Mr. Deasy calls "a woman no better than she should be." The Normans settled Ireland in the name of Henry II, carving up the available land, becoming more Irish than English, leaving behind names like Fitzgerald and Joyce (Joyeux). Thanks to a papal bull, the *"Bos Bovum"* of which so much bitter fun is made in *Ulysses'* "Oxen of the Sun," Ireland was nominally under the English crown, but the invasions and repressions ordered by Elizabeth I, Cromwell, and William of Orange were required to remind the restless natives of this fact.

Partly as a result of the repressions, Catholicism, which was virtually eliminated in England, continued to flourish, though without official recognition, in an Ireland ruled by members of a Protestant establishment which was strongest in the "Orange" north. Politically, the Catholic majority was disenfranchised until the middle of the nineteenth century, but in the eighteenth century it joined in an uneasy alliance with the Protestants and contributed to the abortive revolution of 1798 which ended the Irish Parliament and brought about the Act of Union with England. After further agitation came the enfranchisement of the Catholics (1829), a real victory for an alleged relative of Joyce's father, Daniel O'Connell.[3] A repressed and depressed Ireland with a growing population but no industry, no trade, no self-government, suffered its greatest catastrophe in 1847, when the potato blight brought starvation and emigration, halving the mid-century population and turning the emerald island into a

Celtic Zion. The famine, a result of years of deprivation and English mismanagement, increased unrest, violence, and repression.

Thirty years later, during Gladstone's government, Ireland began to move toward the peaceful attainment of Home Rule. The great leader was an Irish Protestant, Charles Stewart Parnell, who managed to unite the Irish members of the London Parliament as an obstructive body capable of exacting compromises from the ruling party. Irish stubbornness under his brilliant leadership became a powerful weapon. Meanwhile, the Land League, founded by Parnell and Michael Davitt (1879), agitated for land reform using boycotts and occasionally violence, and supported by secret organizations like the Fenians, White Boys, Molly Maguires, and Ribbonmen. Since, for the English, the obstructive Parnell and this violence were one, it is no wonder that the "inevitable betrayer" appeared to forge letters linking Parnell to the political assassinations committed by a group called the Invincibles. Parnell was tried and acquitted, but another betrayer appeared, Captain O'Shea, a Parnell aide and the husband of his long-time mistress. Named in O'Shea's divorce suit, Parnell was deposed as a leader and denounced by the Catholic church. Having suffered at the hands of his former friends and lost the support of the Irish people, he died brokenhearted in a divided country. It was this development (which darkens Stephen Dedalus' first Christmas dinner in *A Portrait of the Artist as a Young Man*) that effectively squelched Home Rule, giving rise to further Fenian agitation, the Irish Language revival, the literary renaissance and the Sinn Fein movement, all of which contributed to the revolution and the "troubles" and led eventually to the establishment of the Irish Free State.

Such are the bare bones of the Irish "nightmare" of history from which the depressed and depleted Stephen of *Ulysses* is "trying to awake." These are the tensions which shaped the Ireland into which Joyce was "lugged," "squealing into life" on February 2, 1882 so that he could grow up, an extraordinary product of the Irish *fin de siècle*. Though it would not do to exaggerate the importance of history in the life of a man who had more in common with the "Irish saints and sages" than with the wild Irish, Joyce too was torn and shaped by conflicting forces: by antagonisms between an international church and a passionate secular nationalism; between an unstable but vital home environment and a stable theological system; between the repressive demands of a culture at once ailing and aspiring and a growing sense of his own worth accompanied by a need to express himself freely; between his strong, pious, long-suffering mother and his wonderfully gifted but profligate father, who accumulated debts and children while leading the life of a Dublin character and always traveled in reasonably good company.

Joyce seems to have inherited from his father, along with a fine tenor voice, a mimic's ear and a love of language that are characteristically Irish, and a truly fine sense of the word. From his mother he derived a respect for the church and things of the spirit. A shy, proud boy, with quick wit but poor sight, he preferred words to actions and written to oral presentation. He quickly found pleasure in books which led him out of Ireland even before he left the Irish church. Joyce's childhood was marred by the steady decline of his father's fortunes which was manifested in a seemingly endless series of quick moves into increasingly depressing homes. Still, apart from a short period spent with the plebeian Christian Brothers, whom Stephen Dedalus so despised,[4] his training was entirely in the hands of the proud and sophisticated Jesuits, who instilled in him a love of ritual and an astonishing mental discipline.[5] His engagement with the church, which doubtless helped him in his pride to support disappointments elsewhere, was so strong that severance left permanent marks. Inevitably, in his books the church is one of a trinity of insidious enemies and obsessive themes: church, home, country. No wonder Joyce makes the prime motive of Stephen's gloom in *Ulysses* his failure to "kneel down and pray" for his dying mother (an event that has only symbolic significance in terms of his biography).

By the time Joyce graduated from Belvedere College and entered University College, literature had begun to serve as a substitute for a priestly vocation. When he graduated from University College in 1902, Ireland and the Irish literary set were already too small for him. He had read widely in continental literature and may even have begun to cultivate the protective mask described in *A Portrait of the Artist as a Young Man* and *Ulysses*. His first major publication, a critical article, "Ibsen's New Drama" (on *When We Dead Awaken*), published in the prestigious *Fortnightly Review* in 1900 while he was still an undergraduate, had established him among his classmates as something of a phenomenon. Drawing heavily on Aquinas, Aristotle, Shelley, Flaubert, and Pater, he had begun to formulate an esthetic that spoke for a discipline in his art equivalent to that of the monk in his belief and helped shape his early work, pointing him toward the later experiments. The actual writing out of that esthetic (reproduced in large measure in *Stephen Hero* and somewhat altered for *A Portrait of the Artist as a Young Man*)[6] took place mainly in Paris where he went ostensibly to study medicine.

After a short hungry stay during which he read Ben Jonson and Aristotle and picked up current fads, he was called back to Dublin in April 1903 to his mother's deathbed. (She died of cancer in August, almost two months after the day of *Ulysses*.) Still hungry, Joyce remained in Dublin to witness her interminable decline, writing, teaching, carousing with his friends, quarreling with his father, and courting Nora Barnacle, the semiliterate waitress who later became his wife. Always a date-fetishist (his books characteristically appeared on his birthday, February the second), he memorialized the day of his first date with Nora, June 16, 1904, as the day of *Ulysses*. It was during this transitional period that, casting about like Stephen for means of support, Joyce took singing lessons and even performed in several concerts, failing to win the gold medal at the Irish Festival of Music or Feis Ceoil only because he could not sight read. Finally, in October, after a short wild stay in the Martello tower with Oliver St. John Gogarty, Joyce ran off with Nora to Zurich and settled with her in Trieste. He had promised his friends to produce a novel in fifteen years, one which would surely not make him popular in Dublin.[7] Though he returned for two brief turbulent visits (1909, 1912), Joyce was effectively in permanent, self-imposed exile.

Before leaving Ireland the second time, Joyce had published, under the pseudonym Stephen Daedalus, the first three of his laconic but biting stories for *Dubliners*. He had also composed poems for his first book, *Chamber Music*, fluty love songs in the Elizabethan manner inspired partly by Ben Jonson but probably also by the French *décadent* poet Paul Verlaine. Both songs and tales jibed with the tastes of the Dublin literati though neither suggested the direction his later work would take. More important was the biographical essay "A Portrait of the Artist," written early in 1904 and refused for publication by the editor of *Dana*, John Eglinton, who was unwilling to print anything he could not understand. The refusal was fortunate, for Joyce turned then to the second and immensely more elaborate version which he continued to work on during the first two years of his European exile. *Stephen Hero*, as this work in progress was ironically entitled, was a detailed and largely factual account of Joyce's own development. Its protagonist was given the name of the "fabulous artificer" Daedalus, who built the labyrinth for King Minos of Crete and later escaped the island on wings of wax and feathers. Stephen is predestined by his nature to become such a figure, the elaborator of great and original literary work, but at this point he is more like Icarus, a clumsy but gifted fledgling, too eager to try his wings.

In 1904, when he left Ireland, where he had suffered poverty and ego damage but failed to make much of a mark, Joyce was already on his way as a writer. Nevertheless, it was his faith in himself that sustained him during the early years of his exile in Trieste where he eventually summoned three members of his family (his brother Stanislaus and two of his sisters). There, while teaching English at the Berlitz school or giving private lessons, he published *Chamber Music* with help from Arthur Symons, finished *Dubliners* (in 1907), and fought the publishers and printers, who persisted in finding objectionable material in the stories, which were finally published in 1914 after many alarms and skirmishes. In 1907, after abandoning *Stephen Hero*, Joyce began rewriting his youth as *A Portrait of the Artist as a Young Man*, a highly stylized, internally focussed and richly symbolic *Bildungsroman*. For all of this activity and despite his frustrations and straitened means, these were tranquil years given over to hard and fruitful work and to the raising of two children, Georgio and Lucia.

In the crucial year 1906, during a brief unhappy interlude as a bank clerk in Rome, which he hated as much as he seems to have loved Trieste, Joyce had an idea. He would write a story for *Dubliners* about a traveling man named Hunter, a Dublin Jew whose wife was said to be unfaithful.[8] Had it been written then, "Ulysses" would have been a slight and probably satirical outsider's view of the "seventh city of Christendom," certainly not an experimental earth shaker. Still, *Ulysses* can be thought of as the last and greatest tale in *Dubliners*, the full-scale portrait designed to convey the beauty and squalor of a city to which the writer could not return but which he could never get out of his head.

In 1915, during World War I, Joyce left Austro-Hungarian Trieste for neutral Switzerland. During the previous year and almost simultaneously, he had completed *A Portrait of the Artist as a Young Man*, begun *Ulysses* and written his play *Exiles*. The latter treats, somewhat in the vein of Ibsen, the return of a writer very much like Joyce to an Ireland that has previously disowned him but now recognizes his success. The play is mainly concerned, however, with the willed but problematical cuckolding of the returned writer, Richard Rowan, by his best friend and admirer, the journalist, Robert Hand. Designed to shock a turn-of-the-century audience with its moral and sexual audacities, it is poor theatre, overloaded with symbolic and thematic significance, full of wooden dialogue and lush ambiguities, and peopled by unconvincing characters. But it is as hard to imagine Joyce writing *Ulysses* without first having written this play as it is to think of *Ulysses* as preceding *A Portrait of the Artist as a Young Man.*

Joyce wrote *Ulysses* largely during the war years in Zurich. During this period and, thanks mainly to the good offices of Ezra Pound, he had already begun to make his reputation through the serial publication of *A Portrait of the Artist as a Young Man* in an English magazine, *The Egoist* (formerly *The New Free Woman*), edited by two ladies, one of whom, Miss Harriet Weaver, became his lifelong patroness. After the war, he stayed first in Trieste, where he shared cramped quarters with his brother Stanislaus (a former confidant and one of the models for the anti-Stephen figures). Later he moved to Paris, where, thanks again to Pound, he was almost immediately a celebrity. *Ulysses* was completed while the family shifted from room to Paris room between 1920 and 1922. In the meantime, however, it had begun to appear serially, first in the American *Little Review* and then in *The Egoist,* and had attracted enough attention to be banned in America and England. Its thirteenth chapter, "Nausikaa," was apparently simple enough for the censors to understand. For ten years after its first publication under the imprint of Sylvia Beach's Paris bookstore, Shakespeare and Co., *Ulysses,* a *succès de scandale,* was smuggled into the States by thrill-seeking tourists. Paradoxically (or properly), the book with Molly in it had prospered in the hands of emancipated women. As Joyce puts it in *Finnegans Wake,* things haven't been the same since "Biddy Doran," the hen scratching up filth in a kitchen midden, "looked ad literature." [9]

By 1933, when Judge Woolsey wrote his landmark decision lifting the ban,[10] the world was ready to accept his experiments, but Joyce had already put eleven years' work into a new and more outrageous project. His greatest book, the puzzling "Work in Progress" (finally published as *Finnegans Wake*) began to appear in Paris periodicals in 1924. For nearly eighteen years, during which he was repeatedly operated on for the eye ailment glaucoma, Joyce elaborated like a true latter-day Daedalus a book without beginning or end, with endless strands of meaning and limitless associative possibilities, burrowing, it would seem, deep into the texture of his own psyche to uncover a vast area of shared experience based on the universal nature of each individual moment and the risibility of the human tragedy. When he finally published it in February 1939 (on his birthday), the world was too busy with Hitler to notice what had happened to literature or to see itself in Joyce's polished mirror. After a tedious struggle to get his family into Switzerland and away from the war, the writer died in Zurich of the complications following an ulcer operation.

II

Joyce's place was already established with the publication of *Ulysses*, but the significance and stature of that book are still being assessed, its sources and influence disputed. Despite the miles and miles of words written about it, it still defies definition, remaining open to each new reader and susceptible to new approaches. We can spot its sources all over the literary map, but it belongs properly to the Flaubertian tradition of literary craftsmanship which was created out of what Joyce called the "classical temper." It reflects a marriage of the Romantic tendency toward vivid and personal expression and the need to universalize and polish that expression, to create autonomous works in which the form is totally adequate to the matter and ordinary life provides a suitable challenge for the artist. In this as in every other way Joyce goes further than his predecessors in expressing uncompromising honesty and an ironic sensibility, and in paying meticulous attention to detail and careful management of esthetic distance. (It is incidentally precisely these qualities which have won Joyce enemies among the anti-esthetic camp, the admirers of writers like D. H. Lawrence or Henry Miller.) No one before him had been so frank in his treatment of the mental and the physical man, so serious, so unromantic and so unlecherous. No one had concerned himself with the unexceptional with quite so much grace, intelligence, and ingenuity. Joyce presents in *Ulysses* a surface that is completely and devastatingly recognizable but which points relentlessly to a deeper sort of recognition, and insists on the universals underlying the objectively presented particulars. Beneath his humor and irony, the trivia of the existences he depicts and the multiplicity of his effects is an unflagging and undogmatic faith in the human potential and a joy, mixed with equal amounts of sorrow and disgust, in the manifold aspects of our experience. Beyond this is the imaginative vitality of a man in love with words and engaged by the literary traditions with and against which he works.

Of course Joyce saw the turning century, lived through World War I and watched distractedly, but with an eye out for raw materials, the liberated twenties which in their turn ushered in inflation, depression, and fascism. But little in his books would suggest that his post-1912 experiences did more than confirm him in his creative direction. In *Finnegans Wake*, in many ways the most personal of his novels, he presents profiles of friends and family, makes reference to the facts of his own later biography, to the literary history of his time, and the current history of Ireland; yet increasingly we sense a detachment from world events and a commitment to the revision of the not-too-distant past. Given the fact that each of his books suggests a different age of man and fresh depths of experience, it is almost as though Joyce had grown old in Dublin, in 1904, the year of his frozen mirror.

If apparently the world was doing little to effect his shape while he was making literary history, he was never completely isolated from literary events, least of all during his formative years. A product, despite himself, of the Irish nineties, he was marked by the Dublin literary movement which he dismissed as provincial—saying in an early essay[11] that George Moore was in a backwater of the realistic movement; spurning Yeats in his Hibernian phase while admiring him as a poet; rejecting the Abbey Theatre as nationalistic; and testing and rejecting the theosophists whom Stephen so cleverly mocks in *Ulysses*: "Through spaces smaller than red globules of man's blood they creepycrawl after Blake's buttocks into eternity of which this vegetable world is but a shadow." (186) For all of this was somehow infected by the genuine vigor of a literary atmosphere which was, after all, not wholly provincial. AE (George Russell), like Yeats, popularized an international and archaizing mysticism. Moore and Yeats did help publicize in England and Ireland the works of the French symbolists Joyce at one time admired. Moore was a vociferous exponent of realism and naturalism, a follower of Flaubert as well as Zola. Joyce was proud to come from the land of Swift, Sheridan, Goldsmith, Wilde, Shaw, and Yeats, though he may have been jealously afraid that a Padraic Colum, an Oliver St. John Gogarty, or a J. M. Synge would eclipse him in the eyes of others. In Ireland he deliberately cultivated the pose of the European artist, read the proper periodicals, knew the Russian, Italian and French novels, read about and in French symbolism, read Dante, Bruno and D'Annunzio in Italian, learned Dano-Norwegian so that he could read Ibsen in the original, and followed with interest the demise of aestheticism in England. His work reflects all of these tendencies though he wrote entirely out of an Irish awareness, belonged to no movements, steering clear even of Ezra Pound's little band, and, like Flaubert before him, refused to be a *chef d'école*. By the time he began to write, the *fin de siècle* with its wonderful operatic props was something he would react against as did so many of his young contemporaries in France and England; but like Proust, Gide, Claudel and D. H. Lawrence, he couldn't help reflecting his past any more than he could help rejecting it. We cannot laugh away the earnestness of the young Stephen Dedalus in chapter 5 of *A Portrait of the Artist as a Young Man*, though Joyce makes us smile at the passion with which the neophyte executes a period poem or at the pattern of his emotional crises which reflect on tastes the author has long since rejected (just as Stephen bitterly mocks his own naïve preciosity when he describes his "epiphanies" in "Proteus"). Joyce was untouched however by the earnest Edwardians and the more polished early Georgians. And though he could not ignore the aging giant Henry James, he seems to have preferred to read a florid D'Annunzio even before he left for the continent. By 1915, he was too far advanced in his own relatively well-bred experiments to be touched by the more radical and ephemeral explosions of expressionism, dadaism, or even by the surrealism with which his books have so much in common. For Joyce the psychological experiments of the latter were invalid as art. He was proud that every word of his writing could be justified and doubtless doubly proud of the labyrinthine logic required to achieve such justification.

Yet, it is no accident that Joyce wrote, in a Zurich full of political, intellectual, and literary tensions which did not directly affect him, a book that was too modern for the twenties. The point is that, writing increasingly out of himself, he wrote for his contemporaries and reacted as they did to immediate and inescapable pressures. *Ulysses*, a product of his immense detachment from contemporary events, is the inevitable reflection of its times, though fortunately free of the cant that mars products of the programmatic movements. Along with Proust's sprawling *Remembrance of Things Past*, Lawrence's *Sons and Lovers*, Mann's *Magic Mountain* or Döblin's *Berlin Alexanderplatz*, but more emphatically than any of them, it reflects a digested awareness of intellectual earthquakes and of the coming era of the little man. Though perhaps a trifle too self-consciously, it also reflects an encyclopedic knowledge of the writer's craft and literary conventions. It emerged in 1922 the first completely modern European novel, the most radically experimental, and the most thoroughly conventional: the indigestible but delightful literary banquet that followed the thunderclap that signalled the destruction of an era, preparing us for things to come.

Today, unlike the early readers, we are not likely to be shocked by the obscenity in *Ulysses*, which is after all organic to the work and mild in comparison to the greater outrage in the books that followed it. Nor are we apt, since Stuart Gilbert's monumental exegesis, to overlook the analogical structures or complain about its formlessness. On the other hand we have perhaps bent over too far in the direction of tolerance, losing both fun and mystery in the process. It is probably inevitable that each new generation of Joyceans will dig deeper in the text for its thrills, or, reacting as much to critics as to the book itself, speak of *Ulysses* as excessively controlled and cold, or discover unplanned incoherence. We come to *Ulysses* armed with the expectations it made possible and steeled in the school of Freud, Marx, Nietzsche, Frazer, Bergson, to say nothing of their followers and rivals, or of Marshall McLuhan, Norman O. Brown, Norbert Wiener, Herbert Marcuse, and Claude Lévi-Strauss. Yet, though one recent critic insists that Joyce's moral vision is impossibly dated, *Ulysses* is still very modern because, born out of the loss of firm faith in either sanctity, order, or progress, it is not a moral tract but rather a gigantic and perhaps even heroic effort to give esthetic order to the shellbits of our "Humptydump world" immersed in the "nightmare" of history.

III

Though he wrote neither a *roman fleuve* nor any two works in the same mode and though any one of his books may be read and enjoyed separately, Joyce's novels and stories form a complex whole and a comprehensive sequence. Reading them in the order of their composition, we acquire skills and an awareness to correspond in a measure to the artist's own developing and expanding vision which was pushed inevitably toward the communal nightmare of *Finnegans Wake*. (It is characteristic of Joyce that his first preparations for his last book were made under headings drawn systematically from each of his previous works.) Details, characters, events, effects, and techniques from one work carry over into the next much as the image or event occurring in one chapter will turn up in later episodes as a symbol or an echo. Like the thrifty housewife, Joyce used the stock and ingredients from yesterday's soup to flavor today's casserole. Accordingly, Tom Kernan, "that drunken little barrelly man that bit his tongue off falling down the mens WC drunk" (773) in "Grace," bumbles drunkenly on as one of Bloom's foils; and the sticks and birds used to such effect in the *Portrait* are given fresh life in *Ulysses* and extended even into the *Wake*. Since Joyce learned through writing, the technical breakthrough of one book becomes a staple in the next. We cannot begin our descriptive treatment of *Ulysses* without considering briefly the works that it complements and continues.

The autobiographical essay "A Portrait of the Artist" suddenly converted Joyce from aspiring playwright, poet, and critic into a writer of prose fiction. Previously, he had written nothing closer to

serious fiction than a juvenile piece for *Titbits* (68–69), a collection
of sentimental sketches called *Silhouettes* which Richard Ellmann
describes as "avant-garde writing of the school of General Booth," [12]
and of course those delicate records of revealing moments Joyce
called "epiphanies." [13] The "Portrait" essay represented a fresh departure. Written in a mannered, elliptical style that recalls Walter
Pater, J. K. Huysmans, and the poetic extravagance of Gabriele
D'Annunzio, it is full of ironical jabs at his own developing person,
and larded with bits of his aesthetic and with philosophical asides.
Stimulated, perhaps by the tone of Eglinton's refusal, Joyce abandoned this style when he started writing *Stephen Hero*, a rather conventional novel of education despite its unconventional approach to
a hero, at once admirable and fallible, whose life was so closely patterned after the author's that Joyce could affix dates to the chapters
in his outline. (He planned to take Stephen Dedalus from birth
through Paris exile and return.) Seen in relation to *A Portrait*, the
parts of *Stephen Hero* that have survived help illustrate the extent
to which Joyce's command of his means had increased between 1904
and 1907. Here is a competent, even a polished narrative, which sets
its protagonist in a clearly delineated ambiance and treats him with
respect from an ironic remove. There is nothing in this partial
account of the university years which would have astonished readers
of the time, though we may suppose that some of the missing sections
contained graphic accounts of Stephen Dedalus' religious and sexual
experience.

Joyce began writing *Dubliners* when George Russell, impressed
by the bits of *Stephen Hero* he had read, suggested he write a
story for his *Irish Homestead*: something "simple, rural, live-mak-
ing, pathos [pathetic]." [14] Joyce quickly produced "The Sisters," a
first person narrative which conveys through circumstantial details
the reactions of a small boy to the illness and death of a paralyzed
and demented old priest. The boy's essential ignorance, faithfully
preserved in his past tense narrative, puts the burden of understanding on the reader, who is engaged by an intriguing blend of
drama and mystery. Though Joyce did not then know it, this tale,
signed with the name Stephen Daedalus, rendered the manner if not
the conception of *Stephen Hero* obsolete as of the summer of 1904.
The stories that followed, written in what Joyce called a style of
scrupulous meanness and designed to expose to Dublin its own
torpor, are a cross between satire and social criticism. Each tale is a
vignette covering some aspect of the city's life, deftly pointing up
a moral failure which the reader must extricate from the closely
woven texture of the understated circumstance. The shorter form

enabled Joyce to refine his techniques, to evolve among other things a powerful third person narrator capable of adjusting his voice to the character and circumstance and of conveying through calibrated indirection a wealth of implications which the simple surface belies. It was probably the writing of the last and most accomplished tale, "The Dead" (1907), that caused Joyce to scrap the novel. Here he had produced in his most objective voice a multi-personal situation focussed by a flash of recognition, a device he was to modify for the *Portrait*.

Nevertheless, when he decided to rename his novel *A Portrait of the Artist as a Young Man*, Joyce symbolically returned to his original conception, long since lost in the sprawling narrative of *Stephen Hero*. Ruthlessly cutting and doubtless altering the tone and perspective of the sections which now constitute chapters 1 through 3, he projected a five chapter format which would eventually suggest what he had called, in language that echoed his aesthetic theory, the "individuating rhythm" of Stephen's character, "the first or formal relation of [its] parts." [15] The result was something startling and fresh, a new wave of the tide which Joyce had described in 1901 as advancing "from Flaubert through Jakobsen [*sic;* Jens Peter Jacobsen, the Danish author of *Niels Lyhne*] to D'Annunzio." [16] Eliminating everything which did not contribute directly to the development of Stephen's "soul," whose symbolic release at the end of chapter 5 constitutes a second birth, Joyce sacrificed both transitions and the Dublin and home ambiance. The *Portrait* records in interlocking prose vignettes the immediate impact and the underlying pattern of experiences that at once dictated and signaled his hero's growth. The new narrator, ostensibly the objective recorder of Stephen's awareness, is versatile and daring. Not only does he alter the style of each chapter to suggest a similar alteration in Stephen's nature, he also varies his tactics within a chapter. Stephen's first Christmas dinner is rendered as a modified Dickensian narrative that seems to open a window out into the world from his constricted consciousness. His religious crisis is interspersed with a literally transcribed series of sermons on last things, which dominates the pivotal third chapter. The book ends on a note as startling as the record of infant sensations with which it opens: Stephen's diary entries, recorded without comment in their pristine incoherence, signal his coming of age and engage us more immediately than ever in his aspirations while defining his triumph as a romantic illusion.

Already in *Dubliners* Joyce began tentatively introducing suggestive analogies for his protagonists and action. In the *Portrait* where his goal was to create an individual who could serve as an ironic but not unworthy prototype of youthful heroism, he was far more systematic. He established, for example, a recognizable though veiled parallel with the Daedalus and Icarus myth which is expressed not only in terms of Stephen's awareness of his strange name and its connotations, but also through premonitory images. Carefully shaded allusions to birds (at first threatening and then gradually glorious and auspicious) or to figurative labyrinths (dark, narrow streets, hands forming a trap, rivulets meandering across a beach, nets) reflect upon and parallel both the development of Stephen's mind and his changing relationship to the Irish forces shaping him. Such images contribute to parallels that foreshadow the more systematic and numerous though not necessarily less subtle analogies which distract so many readers of *Ulysses* for whom the *Odyssey* parallel is a byword. They must be seen not only as part of the controlling and unifying mechanism but also as a commentary on the hero that is not entirely negative though it is certainly ironic.

While the evolution of the chapter styles in the *Portrait* chronicles a parallel development in Stephen's growing awareness and powers, the deliberately but subtly redundant chapter developments supported by the measured use of significant imagery relate that development to the "curve" of his identity seen as a "fluid succession of presents . . . of which [the] actual present is a phase only." [17] The typical chapter begins with a sentiment of impotence more than borne out by the disillusionments that follow and concludes on a note of new-found power which determines the direction of the next section. Such, Joyce implies, is the pattern of Stephen's life, and accordingly, he wrote *Ulysses* as the sixth chapter of that life, artfully withholding the implied conclusion.

All of this and much more is important to the reader of *Ulysses*, in which Joyce builds on his technical discoveries and in a sense reverses the perspective of the *Portrait*, presenting the individual in terms of the society upon which he reflects and in which he will find his own image. Also significant, of course, is a decision Joyce probably made between 1909 and 1912, to cut off Stephen's development at the moment of his first flight and to combine the next stage of his development with the adventures of Mr. Hunter-Bloom, whose day ends with his irrevocable awareness of his wife's adultery. In this way he drew on an already established counter rhythm, that of Stephen's awareness and of his aspiring youth to complicate and give value to his portrait of the Dublin everyman.

⤳ II ⤳

DUBLIN, JUNE 16, 1904

I

It is convenient to say that *Ulysses* is about a day in Dublin, a day that has become as famous as many historically more significant dates. Under the appearance of exhaustiveness, it manages to present those details which reveal most tellingly the quality of that day. The illusion of completeness is most strongly conveyed in the experiences and reactions of a Dublin everyman-noman, Leopold Bloom, who is perhaps the most particularized character in all literature but who is also, and consequently, among the most generalized. Cast adrift by the accident of his wife's infidelity, but an habitual stranger in the land of his birth, he observes the world with exceptional clarity in spite of his inability to see or assert himself as distinct from it. To this indiscriminate but objective consciousness, Joyce added the selective, subjective, shaping consciousness of Stephen Dedalus, who experiences metaphysical confusion and struggles to establish for himself workable goals and a sense of his identity within a world he is unable to accept, unwilling to apprehend. *Ulysses*, like its principal models (*The Odyssey, The Divine Comedy, Hamlet,* and *Faust*) depicts a man's world, a world of ideas, objects, and actions, but woman provides a background and a focus for male activity. As in *Exiles* and *Finnegans Wake*, a woman has the last word, filling the space of the novel with unfettered musings welling up from secret sources of strength and turning on the nature of maleness which she subsumes.

Generically, there can be no doubt that *Ulysses* is a piece of prose fiction in the novelistic tradition. But that tradition is notoriously heterogeneous, and Joyce's novel is remarkably innovative. The point is not that we should recognize in the brilliant synthesis a new mode or a fresh generic heading but rather that we should understand those qualities that set it apart so that we may better appreciate what it is on its own terms. Joyce has written an omnibook (or at least he has tried to write one and such an attempt is an

15

heroic sort of folly), a book that responds to most of our tags but corresponds to none. Putting his playful intellect to work on a new sort of literary problem—how to convey in its integrity the modern predicament without defining man out of history—he has come up with startling and delightfully fresh literary solutions. It is tempting to play Joyce's own game and coin an absurd term like Stephen's "theolologicophilolological" (205) or Lynch's "Pornosophical philotheology" (432) to describe his accomplishment. But such comical designations, suggesting as they do a hash or an Irish stew (another of Joyce's terms), do more justice to the confused thought of a Stephen Dedalus than to the novel in which he appears. In *Ulysses* many separate voices contribute to a unified and coherent second creation, and we can trace paths through the labyrinth without losing the dramatic narrative they must serve. At any moment the dominant mode (say the farcical in "Circe" or "Cyclops" or the rhetorical in "Aeolus" or the comical in the characterization of Bloom) will derive support from other seemingly antagonistic modes, and frequently, what appear to be abrupt changes are the legitimate fruit of careful modulation and far from inexplicable. While the fates of Stephen, Bloom, and Molly, to say nothing of the other Dubliners, are inextricably entwined, all are ultimately and emphatically distinct. *Ulysses* may well be an *Eintopf*, but if so, it is one of those engrossing Chinese soups, each of whose many ingredients remains magically distinct in a savory broth to which each contributes something indefinable.

Joyce's title, and his systematic use of the homeric and other analogies, point up a much-discussed aspect of *Ulysses*, its status as a modern prose epic, or a mock epic novel. Surely his ambitions were epic. That is, he chose to evoke through a single coherent circumstance and with encyclopedic intensity the quality and spirit of a nation and an epoch. He chose as his protagonists exemplary figures (or rather figures that can be thought of as exemplary) and yet tried to convey the gravity of their personal dilemmas. At the same time he seemingly reversed the prime quality of most epics, choosing to depict antiheroes, apparent failures, preferring the trivial circumstance to the momentous, the irreverent attitude to the reverent, dispensing with harmonious and elevated style and tone. The scope of his narrative is another matter. Homer manages to confine his action to a few days while dealing with a ten-year period. The events he describes take us all over the known world *and* to Hades and Olympus. Dante's internal pilgrimage with its four levels of interpretation takes him in jig time through the earth and into the heavens before depositing him on his own doorstep, depicts him as human and fallible while subjecting him to visions ranging from absolute debasement to absolute elevation. Goethe's *Faust* spans heaven and hell, telescopes history, takes its learned hero through every section of his society in the company of a diabolic clown who may be thought of as an aspect of his own character. Each of these is in some sense a serious epic, a titanic vision in contrast to which Joyce's simple plot and mundane setting is dwarfed unless we take into consideration the detailed analogies, the complexity of his vision, the range of his styles and the fact that he explores as no one else the inner and outer aspects of the human predicament. Ultimately, *Ulysses* stands on the epic scale somewhere between the serious works Joyce pretends to mimic and the comic and mock epics which it resembles in so many of its details: works like Petronius' *Satyricon* with its clownish protagonists, its stylistic verve, and its persistent outrage; Rabelais's *Gargantua and Pantagruel*, which inflates the commonplace and delights in the absurd; and Sterne's *Tristram Shandy*, which turns style and stylist into clownish personae and spoofs the reader's expectations. There is always a serious undertone to Joyce's fun and a comic tinge to his seriousness. He has managed to show the extraordinary as a quality of the ordinary. By altering comic practice, he has made an exemplary norm of the exception and the failure. Systematically working against conventions too numerous to list, he has behaved in a most conventional manner and written a book that is totally rational and coherent, balanced and harmonious.

Though the characterization or rather the exposure of character through action and reaction are very important in *Ulysses*, plot and engrossing action become almost vestigial. In fact they frequently function as they do in Virginia Woolf's *The Waves*, where all of the physical action takes place, so to speak, off stage, and we are given only its reflection in the distorting mirror of the characters' minds. Or again, as in a symbolist poem, the objective universe of *Ulysses* is frequently glimpsed *through the medium* (i.e., the style itself) and *in terms* of it rather than *in* the novel, and our pleasure is drawn from the process of apprehending what happens, the meaning of what happens, and the expression which is in itself an event. In a stream of consciousness passage, for example, we are more interested in the effect of the particulars on the character than in the detail itself until we realize that it too has its functions which ultimately, though often indirectly, add to our sense of action and meaning. Joyce gives us details and actions in solution and obliges us to sort out the givens, reconstitute first the moment, then its effect and significance, and then perhaps return to the detail for new treasures. Under these circumstances plot and even the simplest particulars of the action become rewards for diligent reading, the donkey's carrot which many conscientious readers never quite consume.

This need not invalidate the usual questions, the whats and whys of motivation, but it does make them harder to phrase and answer and it puts such questions elsewhere, if not lower, on the scale of values. As if to emphasize this, Joyce permits apparently trivial details to operate as symbols, forming curious clusters. The motto of a potted meat company, the missing letter on Bloom's hat band ("ha"), the letter left out of his name in the newspaper account of Dignam's funeral ("Boom"), and the lagging sandwichman in the procession spelling out "H.E.L.Y.S." all contribute to our sense of the incompleteness and inadequacy of Bloom's position. Or again, in a lighter and lower vein, we have two female activities constituting the poles of the book or rather opening and closing the circle of its action. In the first chapter Stephen imagines the old milk woman whom he associates with Ireland, "Crouching by a patient cow at daybreak . . . a witch on her toadstool." (13) It is almost 3 a.m. when a lusty Molly Bloom rises from the jingling bed to squat on an "orange-keyed chamberpot," (64, 770) which according to Bloom "has only one handle." (547) Here we find a typical symbolic pleasantry and as neat a symbolic cluster as any in the book. These two female images may suggest life and death interchangeably. The pot is incomplete, recalling not only the inadequacy of the Blooms' relationship but also the image of the "one-handled adulterer," Lord Nelson, whose monument is the site of a wasteland fertility ceremony imagined by Stephen. Bloom, who has left his housekey, the symbol of his functions and of home rule, in Molly's room, spends his day searching for a way to return. Stephen, who must cut loose if he is to actualize his potential, has left behind the impossibly heavy key to the tower which his friend Mulligan calls the omphalos (see the navel of the world and the cord connecting us to the primal and the temporal womb). Orange is the color of the Protestant Lodges of the North and the Protestant establishment controls Catholic Ireland. The simple and useful object on which Molly squats is then also an irreverent symbol for the keys, the omphalos-tower, Home Rule for Ireland, and the female potential.

Joyce handles such details with studied negligence, permits them to play like lights on the surface of the action. He is even more casual with the sort of vital statistics another novelist might deliver into our hands in his first chapter. We must keep our eyes open if we are to find Bloom's age, his marriage date, the jobs he has held and lost. We must piece together Stephen's reasons for leaving his father's house, to say nothing of why he goes to the National Library in "Scylla and Charybdis" or to Horne's lying-in hospital in "Oxen of the Sun." Such details and a host of others are suppressed or glossed over or dropped casually into the flood of facts where they surprise and delight a reader almost as much as the solution to a good mystery. Since nothing of obvious moment happens during *Ulysses* and no one of exceptional stature walks the streets of Dublin during Bloomsday, it is a tribute to Joyce's art that we are intrigued when we find that while in solipsistic anguish Stephen *walks* on the beach in "Proteus," the all-too-relaxed Bloom *sits* on the beach in "Nausikaa." Or again it matters to us as it does to Bloom that Molly has probably been faithful during Bloom's ten years of relative abstinence and that Boylan is probably her first lover, though we have been encouraged up to the last chapter to see her as a monumental whore.[1] For the justification on the naturalistic level of Stephen's hallucinated behavior in "Proteus" and elsewhere, we should know that he needs and lacks glasses, a fact mentioned only in "Circe" where Stephen, who is having trouble lighting his cigarette, remarks, "Must get glasses. Broke them yesterday." (560) Such facts alter our conception of character; others simply increase our enjoyment of the moment, but inevitably as a consequence of Joyce's method, we will miss something, for there is too much to meet the eye and tease the intellect.

II

Since, even on the "realistic" level, *Ulysses* suggests multiple readings, any single account of the plot is bound to include a degree of interpretation that will limit its value by excluding other readings and fixing what is otherwise a fluid circumstance. The following brief summary is my "version" of what happens to the questers during their eighteen hours of equal-opposite peregrination through the phenomenal world toward the silent stasis of the womb and the turbulence of rebirth.

Poor, bedraggled, and still unfledged, Stephen has returned to Ireland from Paris, where he read much but wrote little. A grounded hawk among wild geese, he learned bitterness, disillusionment, and some French, and lost nothing by returning to watch his mother die of cancer. He is a gloomy figure, in mourning as much for his own intransigence at not having prayed at his mother's bedside as for the love he feels unable to replace. Having abandoned a home ill-served by his profligate and quarrelsome father, he has returned to his university environment, renting a Martello tower[2] in which for ten days he has lived riotously with Buck Mulligan. (With encyclopedic thoroughness Joyce has here begun to suggest ironic parallels, seeing, for example, in the Irish literary renaissance confused echoes of the ferment of Renaissance England, the sparkle of the eighteenth century and the brilliance of fifth century Athens. Among other things, he may be playing on the friendship between the young provincial Shakespeare and his cultivated friend Ben Jonson, a relationship that must have tickled his fancy.) A clever poetaster who hobnobs as an equal with the lights, Buck is Stephen's discoverer and initiator, as well as the successor to the dour Cranly of the *Portrait*. It is clear that, like Buck, and despite himself, Stephen still shares with the Irish intelligentsia and the mystics an addiction to the *fin de siècle* spirit, as witness the quatrain he writes on the beach during "Proteus" and quotes in "Aeolus." It is also fairly clear that he feels instinctively dissatisfied with that moment's fading bloom and trapped by an allegiance which has not fertilized his muse. Stephen is still the "artist as a young man," a fact which no amount of cynicism can dispel. To understand the nature of his dilemma we need only read in the poetry of Baudelaire, Mallarmé, and Verlaine, the theatre of Maeterlinck or the derivative poems of Swinburne and Wilde, both of whom Mulligan admires. Such writers, though brilliant, are dangerously accessible to the imitators, the mockers, and the faddists, who seem suddenly to have replaced the philistines as Stephen's foils in Dublin.

Apart from its symbolic echoes, as womb, phallus or oracular omphalos, temple, castle or cell, the tower is an aesthetic image of romantic isolation, a cliché from the past by which Stephen feels trapped. His terrified reaction to Haines's black panther nightmare of the previous night, blending with his own dream-vision of his dead mother as a ghostly presence, is only the immediate source of his statement to Mr. Deasy: "History . . . is a nightmare from which I am trying to awake." (34) Caught, like Goethe's Faust, in a past both distant and recent, he desires to wake into his own present. We may feel that he has not really moved very far since he broke with adolescence on the beach in chapter 4 of the *Portrait*, where the lovely Pre-Raphaelite image of the Bird-Girl threw "open before him in an instant of ecstasy the gates of all the ways of error and glory." [3] But the fact that he seems now to crave another such revelation, one capable of setting him free once more, need not confuse us. He has come a long way along the "curve" of his identity and is perhaps ready for a different sort of initiation by another sort of angel.

At 8 a.m. in the Martello tower Stephen climbs the staircase to speak to the shaving, gesticulating, ebullient, protean Mulligan about Haines's nightmare and indirectly about his own concern with pride and guilt. After brooding on his outrage and shame, he joins the others below where Mulligan, who has fixed breakfast, makes mocking allusions to him as a servant, allusions Stephen takes to his symbol-loving heart and nourishes along with other slights that darken his day. It is not hard to understand Stephen's resentment at being obliged to shine for the greater glory of a man who repeatedly outshines him, though, given his enormous lucidity, it may be hard to appreciate the self-destructive urge and the frustrations that have led him to confide in Buck and the inertia that keeps them together. We may be sure that there is some mystic crux here and that Stephen, ever eager like the German mystic Jakob Böhme to read the "signatures of all things" (37), sees Mulligan as a necessary evil, a needed scourge and goad. "Offend me still. Speak on" (218), he mutters several hours later as they leave the National Library together. It follows then that the old milkwoman who favors the bantering Mulligan is an allegory of Ireland, the Shan van Vocht, or "poor old woman," bowing to false values. Mulligan washing, dressing, undressing, and diving into the "forty foot hole" (or men's swimming area) is for the poorly clad hydrophobe an allegory of guilt and usurpation. Even more painful for one who has lived through his own moment of soaring Daedalian aspirations on the beach in the *Portrait* is the sight of Mulligan's fluttering birdhands as he dives, a graceful but comic Icarus, into the water Stephen fears. Still, at the Buck's insistence, he leaves behind the tower key and twopence for beer and promises to meet him at a pub called The Ship where they will begin spending Stephen's salary and he will elaborate his Shakespeare theory for the well-heeled Haines. Stephen has already decided not to return to the tower: "I will not sleep here tonight. Home also I cannot." But it should not be assumed that he has really made up his mind.

There are large gaps in the action of "Telemachus," despite the meticulous attention to details. For one thing, while Stephen thinks, the action continues. What Stephen overlooks, we too miss. Again, though we watch Mulligan shave, eat, cavort, dress, and finally bathe, we see Stephen performing only minimal actions. We may well feel that his detachment on this level approaches morbid asceticism, an impression Joyce supports throughout the book, permitting us to see him take nothing but liquid refreshment and emphasizing his utter disregard for things of this world, his joyless prodigality. Like Faust, he is an incomplete man, one who has cultivated his spirit at the expense of his flesh and who is now embittered by the quality of his rewards. Perhaps the circumstance of his mother's death, perhaps the failure of his art, perhaps the cool reception given him by the Dublin literary establishment, perhaps his sense of being dragged back into the Irish quagmire he thought he had flown above, perhaps all of these things together have confused and paralyzed him. At any rate (and in this he resembles an Irish Hamlet), he fills those parts of his day we witness with activities designed to disguise his sense of futility but drawing him inevitably closer to a moment of decision.

The hours between 9 and 11 ("Nestor"), of which we see only a fraction, are spent in Deasy's school. There, more engaged by his own historical consciousness than by their evident lack of interest, Stephen catechizes Protestant boys in their lessons and vainly tries to amuse them with a pointless riddle. An inept teacher or "gentleman usher" reenacting his own boyhood and schooling at Clongowes Wood, he feels drawn only to a class weakling. Contemplating this child he sees his own enslavement to a dim personal past and unconsciously predicts the necessary chaos of "Circe": "Secrets, silent, stony sit in the dark palaces of both our hearts: secrets weary of their tyranny: tyrants willing to be dethroned." (28) It is Thursday and a halfday, and as the boys rush out to play (another echo from his past), Stephen switches roles to become the reluctant pupil of the crusty and opinionated and yet fatherly Mr. Deasy. He listens uneasily to anti-Fenian, anti-Semitic and anti-feminist diatribes and receives, with his salary, lectures on history and economy, and a letter on hoof and mouth disease which he promises to deliver to his journalist acquaintances. Torn as he is between his roles (boy-man, Catholic-renegade, Irishman-exile, etc.), Stephen's attitude toward Deasy is too complex to be characterized as "unforced respect." [4] The old man is painfully right in several of his judgments, especially when he states, from a contrary position, opinions that parallel Stephen's own (see chapter 5 of the *Portrait*) about the Irish and their heroes, and when he reminds Stephen of his improvidence and suggests that he has no vocation for teaching. He is both a wise Nestor and a prattling old man, a Polonius, unable to understand that Hamlet-Stephen "has reasons." Their spirited quarrel over the vices of the Jews, the only point which Stephen deigns to dispute, must be seen in the perspective of the "Scylla and Charybdis" discussion of Shakespeare's Semitism and Stephen's nocturnal visit with the unacquisitive commercial failure, Bloom.

Sometime between 11 and 12 ("Proteus"), rather than keep his appointment at The Ship, Stephen sends Mulligan a telegram which suggestively paraphrases George Meredith: *"The sentimentalist is he who would enjoy without incurring the immense debtorship for a thing done."* (199) We do not see him sending the telegram or approaching the beach at Sandymount, but we accompany him as he wanders, uncertain of his immedate goal but at last alone with his myriad thoughts. During this dense chapter he makes a decision or two by default (not to walk out into the sea, not to visit Uncle Richie) and performs one significant action: tearing off some paper from Deasy's letter to write the quatrain inspired by a pair of cocklepickers. But mainly the time is taken up by random musings inspired by the sea, the beach, and his own dim sight: an inner soliloquy astonishingly rich in verbal events and allusions but consistently solipsistic. Desperately limited by his nature and nurture, he is a pathetic and cynical shadow of his naïvely hopeful younger self:

> Reading two pages apiece of seven books every night, eh? I was young. You bowed to yourself in the mirror, stepping forward to applause earnestly, striking face. Hurray for the Goddamned idiot! Hray! No-one saw; tell no-one. Books you were going to write with letters for titles. (40)

In "Aeolus," Stephen's and Bloom's paths first cross as Stephen delivers a copy of Deasy's letter to the barmy editor of the *Weekly Freeman,* a chore we may suspect Stephen accepted partly to kill time, partly to please the old man whom he grudgingly admires. Perhaps too he sees journalism as a way out of his impasse and a source of funds; if so his reaction to Miles Crawford's vague offer of a commission (to write a satirical piece!?) is equivocal. At their best the rhetoricians have nothing to offer him. The lover of language is not apt to be delighted by words of praise uttered by wasted men for the wasted words of Irish public speakers. In stark contrast we have his own offering, the original, inconclusive "Parable of the Plums" inspired by his epiphany of two midwives crossing the beach in "Proteus." The "Parable," recited as Stephen leads the mob to a pub, is received generously but, like the riddle in "Nestor," with incomprehension.

His visit to the pub has left Stephen light-headed and courageous enough to beard the pseudonymous pundits at the National Library ("Scylla and Charybdis"): John Eglinton (Magee), and AE (George Russell). He may have come to the librarian's office in order to put Deasy's letter in AE's hands,[5] but he may also have come in quest of Haines who speaks of the library in "Telemachus." As usual, he is torn between conflicting emotions and aspirations. Despite the ironical asides, he respects Eglinton's Aristotelian rigor and craves both his attention and his approval. As for AE, Stephen's feigned indifference ("Stephen looked down on the wide headless caubeen, hung on his ashplanthandle over his knee.") (192)[6] underscores his resentment at being excluded from the list of Irish literary hopefuls whom, ironically, he neither envies nor respects. Amidst the frustrating entrances and departures in this public place, he expounds his Shakespeare theory to a worthy but unsympathetic and easily distracted audience, attempting to demonstrate to them and to himself that he is both an intellectual and a critic. Halfway through the argument, though not before the departure of AE, Mulligan bursts in to assert his dominion over his friend. His ribald wit provides the comic relief that dampens Stephen's spirits and reaffirms the fact that "Kinch" is miscast as a public performer in an Ireland where the clown and bone setter is valued above the priest of art. If he has come to the library hoping to sell the Shakespeare theory to *Dana*, Stephen is disappointed, but we have the sense that he is beyond hope and that each of his acts is an act of desperation designed to convince him of his own failure and leading towards the violence or suicide hinted at in "Proteus" and "Wandering Rocks."

Stephen's Shakespeare argument may be seen as an intellectual and critical exercise in the then popular biographical vein,[7] a substitute for true creative activity, a set piece. But on this day Stephen has little besides his ready wit to second his claim to public attention and help pay his debts. The difference between the famous esthetics conversation with Lynch in chapter 5 of the *Portrait* and this tense and tendentious argument is another symptom of Stephen's fall. In the *Portrait* a relaxed and self-confident Stephen deliberately chose in the reptilian mocker Lynch the peer least likely to approve or understand his theory. Here, unsure of himself in the presence of experts, Stephen is less systematic, more brilliant, and more vulnerable. Fleshing out his Aristotle ("Unsheathe your dagger definitions.") (186) with the aid of his Jesuit training ("Composition of place. Ignatius Loyola, make haste to help me!") (188) and relying of all things on the techniques used in the hell-fire retreat sermons of the third chapter in the *Portrait*, he is engaged both in a creative activity, that is, in making Shakespeare's milieu and predicament vital in the halls of dead learning, and in a personal and pseudoreligious meditation on the trinitarian nature of the artist's relationship to his person and his creation. Tension is generated not only by his sense of failure but also by the emotional conflicts that have sterilized him and permitted others to usurp his laurels.

At about 3 p.m. ("Wandering Rocks") Stephen leaves the library with Mulligan, whom Simon Dedalus has roundly cursed in "Hades" as "a contaminated bloody doubledyed ruffian . . . His name stinks all over Dublin." (88)[8] They separate when Mulligan goes to meet Haines for tea. As one of the rocks amid which the Lord Lieutenant's cavalcade weaves its way toward the opening of the Mirus Bazaar, Stephen is next seen chatting in Italian with Almidano Artifoni, who urges him to reconsider a decision to give up a possible singing career. Later, he surprises his sister Dilly buying a used French text and sees in her mute admiration a reminder of his own failure. This, plus the view we have of the Dedalus family life, the grinding poverty and the scrounging for crusts, justifies Stephen's melodramatic fear of being submerged by their ruin: "She is drowning. Agenbite. Save her . . . She will drown me with her, eyes and hair." (243)

We can assume from the various accounts of Stephen's finances (see for example pages 556–59), that he spends the rest of his day wandering aimlessly and not entirely alone. It is 10 o'clock when Bloom finds him at the Holles Street hospital ("Oxen of the Sun") where Mulligan has promised to meet him after the literary evening at George Moore's house. Brilliantly drunk, Stephen is carousing with medical johnnies and professional parasites, trading puerile quips, elaborating clever conceits and blaspheming, while, upstairs, Mrs. Mina Purefoy is painfully and belatedly delivered of her nth infant. The group is joined by Bloom and later by Mulligan, who as usual dominates the talk and dampens Stephen's spirits. After the birth, the noisy group spills out into the street, recently watered by a frightening and perhaps fructifying thundershower, for a final drink at Burke's pub where Stephen, as usual, treats.

In the drunken confusion after pub-closing at 11 p.m., Mulligan and Haines[9] give Stephen the slip (perhaps after an argument):

> Where's the buck and Namby Amby? Skunked? Leg bail. Aweel, ye maun e'en gang yer gates. Checkmate. King to tower. Kind Kristyann will yu help, yung man hoose frend tuk bungalo kee to find plais whear to lay crown off his hed 2 night. (427)

Stephen, who has silently lusted all day, takes Lynch to Bella Cohen's brothel only to learn that his favorite whore, the clergyman's daughter Georgina Johnson, has married a traveling man. (561) Through most of "Circe," while Bloom watches protectively, he prates scholarly gibberish and barely comprehensible theory, hallucinating mildly while Lynch plays sardonic whetstone. Finally, he breaks out of his torpor into a wild dance which occasions the gruesome but saccharine vision of his dead mother, emblem of the force that has brought him back from Paris and now refuses to release him from Ireland, absolve him of his guilt, and remove his fear of death.

Stephen hysterically rejects her melodramatic claims and accusations and then dispels her image by attacking with his ashplant the mauve lampshade. Dashing out into the street, leaving the vigilant and fatherly Bloom to settle with the whoremistress, he inadvertently offends a British tommy in the course of an absurd altercation during which he hallucinates about England in the shape of Edward VII and Ireland as Old Gummy Granny, both of whom he loudly but incoherently rejects. In the end he is knocked unconscious by a clumsy blow from the uncomprehending private but protected by Bloom who revives him and then encourages him "in orthodox Samaritan fashion" (613) ("Eumaeus") to come along for refreshments.

It is after 1 a.m. when they stop at the cabman's shelter supposedly run by an ex-Invincible and drink undrinkable coffee while a garrulous sailor spins drunken lies. This is the moment Joyce has so carefully prepared us for, when his Ulysses discloses his identity to his Telemachus. We watch expectantly for the marks of recognition, but Stephen, still groggy from the blow and perhaps still a bit drunk, seems more willing to speak to a sponging Corley, whom he mockingly sends to Deasy after his own job, than to Bloom. In "Nestor," he defended the Jews in the abstract for qualities he later discovered in his Shakespeare. Here, in the company of an individual, he finds not the homeless mysterious wanderer but a wandering commonplace on his way home. If the two make contact, it is on the level of music and the songs Stephen sings as they walk arm in arm toward number 7 Eccles Street. After all Stephen has discovered in Bloom a degree of strangeness:

> Accordingly he passed his left arm in Stephen's right and led him on accordingly.
> —Yes, Stephen said uncertainly, because he thought he felt a strange kind of flesh of a different man approach him, sinewless and wobbly and all that. (660)

We are reminded of earlier references to Cranly's and Mulligan's arms and subtly aware that Stephen's sensation might signal a real change in his condition after the rite of passage into the night that is "Circe." However, though Stephen implicitly wishes to be initiated, like Shakespeare, by an older woman (see "Scylla and Charybdis" (191): "And my turn? When?") and though he has probably overheard Dixon's remarks about Molly's charms and availability (425.16–24), he does not seem attracted by the idea of giving Molly lessons on an exchange basis. Having rejected the claims of one mother, he is doubtless unwilling to take on another. In "Ithaca," from which emotions and reactions are systematically excluded, he drinks Epp's cocoa, exchanges a few opinions, and politely refuses an invitation to spend the night. But before the "centrifugal departer" leaves the "centripetal remainer," in a ceremonial gesture common to members of the canine species, the two men mingle their waters in the already watered wasteland garden. Stephen, whose destination is unspecified, has made no great effort to endear himself to Bloom. Rather, he has been gently if acidly humorous and even playful enough to sing an anti-Semitic song to his embarrassed but tolerant semi-Semitic host. There will be no sequel to this visit.

— III

If, from the point of view of Joyce's readers, Stephen is prolonging an already established curve, his equal-opposite comes to us fresh and strange through that grand opening sentence of "Calypso": "Mr Leopold Bloom ate with relish the inner organs of beasts and fowls." (55) He is the very substance of the Old Testament smoke-eating "Jehovah, collector of prepuces" (201) though somewhat softened by the passage of the centuries. Bloom's day is a complete life: past, present, and probable future. Joyce builds him gradually through the memories and reactions of others as well as through his own memories and sensations, delightful as they are trivial, served warm with a seasoning of life and laced with laughter. Putting the facts together, we find that he is thirty-eight years old, the son of an Hungarian Jewish immigrant who changed his name from Virag and married an Irish woman. His recollection of Virag's suicide combined with a sense of having abandoned or lost the traditions of his fathers, reflects in a lighter vein Stephen's distress over his mother's death, and his gnawing "agenbite of inwit." He has married Molly Tweedy, the daughter of an Irish Major stationed on Gibraltar and a Spanish Jewess of questionable morals. They have had a daughter, Milly, fifteen, now a photographer's assistant in the market town of Mullingar, and a son, Rudolph, named after his grandfather, but dead at eleven days, eleven years ago. Intelligent, but untrained and only moderately gifted, Bloom is not a good provider. Having been a peddler of trinkets, a traveler for blotting paper, a clerk in a slaughter house, and, in hard times, a salesman for the "Royal Hungarian Lottery," he now makes a meager living canvassing for ads for the *Weekly Freeman*.[10] As Madame Marion Tweedy, Molly helps support the family with her singing, and is currently planning a tour with Blazes Boylan as her manager. Since the death of their son,

which was traumatic for both of them, Bloom and Molly have had
virtually no sexual relations. Molly seems to have gone her own way
and is now beginning what appears to be her first affair with the
"Worst man in Dublin," (92) as Bloom calls Boylan. Recently, instead of renewing normal relations, Bloom has advertised for a
mistress. Under the pseudonym Henry Flower, he is now corre-
sponding with a lovelorn typist, who signs herself Martha Clifford.
He is, however, thoroughly monogamous. Molly was and is his great
romance: the seduction on the Hill of Howth, like Shakespeare's
seduction in a rye field, remains the sensual event of his life. A diffi-
dent and abstemious man in convivial and bibulous Dublin, Bloom
has many acquaintances but few friends. Though he belongs to the
Masons[11] and hence partakes of a secular mysticism (see, by way of
contrast, Stephen's esoteric preoccupations), he makes little of that
association and less of his prior commitments to Protestantism and
Catholicism, to say nothing of the Judaism into which he was born
but apparently not initiated. Moderate in everything, except perhaps
his secret lusts, he enters *Ulysses* as the thoroughly eclectic and
vaguely sympathetic man in a city full of quirky individuals, a man
who sips cautiously the cup of life, taking care not to swallow too
many bubbles. Altogether, he is a worthy successor to the numerous
nineteenth-century antiheroes and especially to Charles Bovary,
whose miseries and joys are scamped in Flaubert's account of the
philandering Emma.

Bloom's day begins with an 8 a.m. breakfast at 7 Eccles Street
("Calypso"), a very ordinary Dublin address, the former home of
Joyce's friend Byrne, the "Cranly" of the *Portrait*. While Molly lies
upstairs in old man Cohen's jingling bed which her husband believes Major Tweedy brought back from Gibraltar, Bloom buys a
breakfast kidney at the Jewish pork butcher's, serves her coffee, and
gets the mail which contains, along with a letter to him from Milly,
a note to Molly from Boylan, who is coming to see her at 4:00 in
the afternoon. This note and this knowledge keep Bloom away from
home till 2 a.m. Unlike Stephen, who must decide whether or not to
return to Mulligan and the tower, Bloom must decide when to
return to Molly. After breakfast, he goes to the garden privy, where
he reads and then wipes himself with a prize story in *Titbits*, an
emblem of his literary ambitions. Like Stephen, but for this day
only, Bloom is in mourning and keyless. Having changed his suit so
that he can attend the funeral of little Paddy Dignam of the red
nose, he inadvertently leaves his keys in Molly's room.

"Lotus Eaters" finds Bloom at 10 o'clock in another part of town
on his way to the baths. His actions and reactions reflect the coming

euphoria. As Henry Flower, he picks up and eventually reads a teasing letter with a flower enclosure from Martha Clifford. He tells the cadger, M'Coy, about his wife's tour and promises to sign him in at the funeral. He buys some soap for his bath and orders some lotion for Molly and inadvertently gives Bantom Lyons a tip on the horse Throwaway in the Gold Cup race. Finally, to kill time, he drops in to watch a mass with cool and comic objectivity. At 11 o'clock ("Hades"), he joins the funeral party and crosses town to Glasnevin cemetery in a carriage with Simon Dedalus, Martin Cunningham, and John Power, for whom he is clearly an outsider. During the ride he sees Stephen on his way to the beach and points him out to a barely civil Simon, who turns the youth into an object of Bloom's fatherly concern. After the ceremony he tells one of Molly's rejected admirers, the pompous John Henry Menton, that he has a dint in his hat, only to be rudely ignored. This action parallels not only the behavior of Ajax' ghost toward Ulysses but also the gracious thank you Bloom received years earlier when he picked up Parnell's hat.

Bloom turns up next at the drafty *Freeman* office ("Aeolus"), where he is negotiating the terms and layout for an ad for the House of Keyes. We see him only briefly and share few of his thoughts and words in this chapter, which is dominated by the journalistic grubs. Rushing back and forth, suffering minor indignities, and winning minor concessions from busy pressmen and the cantankerous editor, he is curtly rebuffed when he interrupts the pub-pilgrimage to ask for one final favor. All in all he cuts a figure of comic competence in a world of empty words and sham concerns: "Time someone thought about [easing the pains of childbirth]," thinks the ever-considerate canvasser reacting against the rhetoric, "instead of gassing about what was it the pensive bosom of the silver effulgence. Flapdoodle to feed fools on." (161)[12] In "Lestrygonians," between 1 and 2 p.m., Bloom's thoughts turn on food and disgust as he searches for a suitable place to eat. Rejecting Burton's Restaurant where the masticating horde turns his stomach, he settles on Davy Byrne's pub. There he finds a flea-bitten admirer in Nosey Flynn. Earlier he has met a former flame, Josie Powell Breen, married now to the dotty Denis whose behavior gives us a foretaste of Bloom's moon-madness in "Circe." Unlike those who grudgingly applaud Stephen, Bloom's admirers are a curious lot, whose admiration springs from ignorance rather than understanding and whose presence and praise is an embarrassment to him and to us. After his snack, Bloom wanders toward the National Library, a keyless man in quest of copy for the Keyes ad. On his way he helps a blind stripling across the street, a gesture that foreshadows his meeting with the weak-eyed Stephen. Finally he dodges into the museum opposite the library to avoid meeting Boylan: "Straw hat in sunlight. Tan shoes. Turnedup trousers. It is. It is." (183) During the Shakespeare argument in "Scylla and Charybdis," where Stephen sketches a Bloomlike bard, Bloom is part of the background. Only Mulligan, who has just seen him in the museum investigating the hinder parts of a Venus, notes his presence. Bloom's great moment comes when he sails out of the library between Buck and Stephen in an innocent parody of the mythical escape. We see him briefly in "Wandering Rocks" purchasing pornography for Molly. Neither he nor Stephen is included in the catalogue of watchers at the end of this chapter. Both have begun to melt into the crowd.

Shortly before 4 p.m. ("Sirens"), he drops in at the Ormond Hotel bar during a wary and curiously sensual pursuit of Boylan, whose visit to Molly shames and subconsciously pleases him. Sad and lonely, his head filled with thoughts of Molly, he lunches on liver and cider in the company of Stephen's uncle Richie Goulding and stealthily writes a note to Martha. For much of this time Bloom is orchestrated into the musical texture of "Sirens," where the foreground is occupied by flirtatious barmaids to whose charms he is generally deaf but into whose orbit are drawn brilliant performers (siren singers) like Simon Dedalus and Ben Dollard, the unfrocked priest Father Cowley, the sly cadging Lenehan, and of course dashing Blazes Boylan, who quickly departs in his hired cab but whose jingling progress we follow to his goal. True to his word in the *Exiles* notes, Joyce has made the seducer an insipid if flashy fancyman, a powerful but unworthy rival, as Molly's reactions in "Penelope" indicate. Boylan, the carefree conqueror, represents the world of trivial business deals, sporting life, pub talk, and casual alliances. He is appropriately seen in transit and conveniently dismissed to remain a presence only in the minds of other characters and a reproach to Bloom.

It is 5 o'clock ("Cyclops") when Bloom, keeping an appointment to help settle the affairs of Dignam's widow, stations himself in front of Barney Kiernan's pub. Here the focus is on the assorted drinkers gathered around a broken down "patriot" who calls himself "citizen" and glories in his and Ireland's past. Much against his wishes, Bloom is dragged into the group which knows him as a freemason and a Jew and suspects him of having won on Throwaway, a twenty-to-one bet at the Ascot Races. (325) His failure to buy anything for the thirsty cadgers (or accept anything but a "knock-me-down cigar") combines with his oppressive reasonableness in this den of unreason or false reasoning to provoke an anti-Semitic eruption. Bloom's last

gesture is a gallant defense of the Jews, among whom he numbers the
son of an apostate (Mendelssohn), apostates (Marx and Spinoza), a
gentile (Mercadante) and of course Jesus Christ. It prompts the irate
and drunken citizen-Cyclops to throw a biscuit tin in the direction
of the departing cab in a scene that foreshadows Stephen's street
brawl in "Circe."

For all the minutiae in *Ulysses,* and despite the completeness of
Bloom's characterization, mercifully, much is left to our imagina-
tions. We share his thoughtstream for only a handful of the day's
hours and in relatively few chapters. Though he defecates and
urinates before us, he shaves, dresses and bathes offstage. We accompany him neither to Keyes's shop where he conducts business nor
to Mrs. Dignam's house where he discusses insurance. Though the
missing details may be tucked into his revery, there is little room
for redundancy in a book where every gesture bears on character
and theme. Mulligan's shaving, dressing, and bathing must suffice for
Bloom as well. It is fitting then that, after two blank hours, Bloom
appears on Sandymount Strand at 8 p.m. ("Nausikaa"). There he
watches the flirtatious behavior of Gerty MacDowell, a coy virgin
in her early twenties, nourished on lady's periodical literature. During Gerty's deliberately but archly seductive leg-swinging performance, Bloom is silent, the distant stranger of her sentimental dream.
His own performance is reflected through her monologue by a sugary
shock of pleasure and shame. In the second half of the chapter we
shift our field and see the departing Gerty through Bloom's objective eyes as he straightens out his clothes and contemplates but
rejects the idea of repeating the experience. The masturbation during the fireworks display for the Mirus Bazaar, a sunset ceremony
(that follows the celebration of the Virgin in a neighboring church!),
partially explains his abstinence in "Circe."

Having dozed off briefly on the beach, but still unwilling to risk
an encounter with Boylan, Bloom goes to the Holles Street hospital
("Oxen of the Sun") to enquire about Mina Purefoy, who is still in
childbirth. Dixon, the young intern who once dressed a bee sting
for him, draws him into the anteroom. There he sits, uncomfortably
abstemious, among the clever young sports, and there he sees the
young student (Madden) who is Milly's first boyfriend. Among the
barflies at Kiernan's he was out of place but intellectually superior.
Here, the unwitting or good-natured butt of witticisms and the
victim of Mulligan's veiled hostility, he is beyond his intellectual
depth. Concerned over Stephen's drunken condition, he follows him
to Burke's pub and then to nighttown.

What actually occurs to him in "Circe" is simple but muzzy for the reader who must attend not only to events but to illusions. Joyce involves us from the start in the hallucinated context, generating through his stage directions a dream landscape out of the most banal materials of nether Dublin. Furthermore, he plunges us into not one but two overwrought psyches artfully interrelated. Yet, we can generally distinguish between the conscious and the subconscious events. Bloom's subvocal hallucinations, which never contribute to the action, begin when he first recognizes his "Brainfogfag." They accelerate during a series of comic, imaginary encounters with his father, with Molly, with Josie Breen, and finally with two members of the watch. Out of this last encounter is generated the first major sequence, Bloom's farcical trial for shame. (457) All of this occurs as the confused canvasser chases after Stephen and Lynch, whom he lost when he dodged into a shop. The sound of "church music" draws him to Bella Cohen's house, where he is propositioned by Zoe, whose request for a cigarette prompts him to begin a lecture that quickly turns him on again. This second and more extravagant hallucination gives Bloom a chance to play the benefactor of mankind and to suffer martyrdom at the hands of the inquisition. Clearly an extension of his pronouncement on brotherly love in "Cyclops," it concludes with a litany of Bloom's adventures sung by the "Daughters of Erin" as Bloom is burned "mute, shrunken, carbonized."

> Kidney of Bloom, pray for us.
> Flower of the Bath, pray for us.
> Mentor of Menton, pray for us.
> Canvasser for the Freeman, pray for us.
> Charitable Mason, pray for us.
> Wandering Soap, pray for us.
> Sweets of Sin, pray for us.
> Music without Words, pray for us.
> Reprover of the Citizen, pray for us.
> Friend of all Frillies, pray for us.
> Midwife Most Merciful, pray for us.
> Potato Preservative against Plague and Pestilence,
>   pray for us. (498–99)

A few moments later Bloom enters the brothel where he finds Stephen by the pianola. He continues to hallucinate mildly until the appearance of the whoremistress, whom he imagines in the shape of a masterful Bello and to whom he joyfully submits in the wildest and most degrading of his visions, being turned in his imagination into something approximating one of Circe's pigs. This grotesque, absurd and obscene sequence concludes with the sound of a snapping trouser button after a mawkish interlude with Bloom's muse, the calendar-art nymph on his bedroom wall. Virtually restored and saved from the depths of himself, Bloom has a final relatively mild hallucination, participating in Boylan's seduction of Molly as an exaggerated version of that comic byword, the complacent husband. The whole experience, though it dominates the chapter, has taken relatively little time, but it has steeled Bloom for what is to come: the encounter with Stephen and his return to Molly's bed. Having capitulated to impulses that crippled him, he is free to resume a role that is both dominant in him and appropriate.

As Bloom emerges from his last hallucination, Lynch makes the equation that signals a transfer of our attention to Stephen, pointing to the mirror in which both are joined in the likeness of Shakespeare under the antlered hatrack. (567)[13] Stephen, who begins by raving incoherently, spewing out the garbled contents of the day's thoughts, finally breaks into his drunken dance and begins hallucinating aloud. Having previously taken Stephen's money in safe keeping (seconding in this the advice of old Deasy, his precursor, and inverting the behavior of the pawnbroker Dodd, his dark reflection), a masterful Bloom pays the damages after the attack on the lampshade and runs out into the street. He arrives too late to prevent the fight, but still manages to fend off the police while Stephen lies in a drunken stupor. It is at this point that the symbolic link between the two men is confirmed by Bloom's version of Rudy as an eleven-year-old Pre-Raphaelite dream child with a "mauve" face, a ghastly-sweet emanation hovering over the prostrate poet. The moment is worthy of the Dublin Christmas Pantomime, but the reader may be moved as well as amused and shocked.

Concerned and eager to help, anxious to make contact with the youth he has identified with his son, Bloom escorts the sodden bard to the nearby cabman's shelter for undrinkable coffee and an inedible bun. Thanks to the presence of a returning sailor who spins improbable traveler's tales, conversation is difficult if not impossible. Still, for the first time this day, Bloom is in command of the fate of another whom he respects and, though tired, he is more than usually alert and talkative. Stephen, by contrast, distracted and bored, speaks rarely and at cross purposes with Bloom. Seizing on the fact that his protégé has eaten nothing for over a day (656), Bloom decides to offer him a bed for the night and brave Molly's wrath. As they walk home together Stephen warms to a discussion of music and begins singing, inspiring the practical-minded Bloom to outline the advantages of a musical career. During the song, the older man completes the transition to fatherhood by echoing in milder and muddier terms Simon Dedalus' opinion of Mulligan's influence:

> ... he purposed (Bloom did), without anyway prying into his private affairs on the *fools step in where angels* principle advising him to sever his connection with a certain budding practitioner, who, he noticed, was prone to disparage, and even, . . . with some hilarious pretext, . . . deprecate him. . . . (664–65)

In response to this, a horse mires and Stephen maunders about "usurpers."

At 7 Eccles Street ("Ithaca"), Bloom shows Stephen into the kitchen, makes two cups of cocoa, lacing Stephen's generously with Molly's breakfast cream, a further sign of new-won independence. Their conversation turns on their common backgrounds, their differences, and the similarities that underlie them (see the delightful equation of the Jewish and Irish traditions). (688) It is only after Stephen has sung his anti-Semitic ballad that the "secret infidel" Bloom offers him a bed and accepts his refusal. After Stephen's departure through the gate, unlocked by an "aruginous male key," Bloom must face the facts he has been avoiding. This he does in the fashion of a returned wanderer, taking inventory first of his worldly situation, inspecting documents that relate his past, observing the evidence of another's usurpation, and deciding what is to be done about it (nothing). Brushing the remains of Boylan's picnic from his bed, he kisses Molly's rump, gives her a slightly modified account of his day, and lies down head to her feet to sleep, a wary much-traveled Sinbad. He has asked her to "get his breakfast in bed with a couple of eggs" (738) and mentioned a possible future association with Stephen. Joyce's "Gea-Tellus," the great mother to whose womb Bloom returns, then begins the musings out of which, for all his failings, the returned traveler emerges her man, the one to whom she has once said, "Yes."

IV

The male world of Stephen and Bloom is characteristically incomplete ("What is a house without Plumtree's Potted Meat" reads the insistent ad). Enclosed all day by the four walls of her house and room, served by Bloom and an inefficient servant, acted upon more than acting, a presence, an emanation but a mastering force as well, Molly complements our sense of the two men, helps to unite them.

Throughout his day Stephen behaves as though everything is an aspect of his self, and his soul is indeed the Aristotelian "form of forms." Bloom, on the other hand, sees himself in relation to the world, while Molly, completing the trinity, perceives the world as relating to her. In her devastatingly frank monologue she reveals herself as *das ewig Weibliche,* but as such she is a product of the male imagination as well as a person in her own right. We are right to see her as the great whore even though she rejects the role and seems in fact to have indulged in nothing more than harmless flirtations during Bloom's long sexual absence. Curiously, it is Molly, fresh from Boylan's embraces, who testifies to Bloom's sexual prowess and rehabilitates him in our eyes, but paradoxically, it is the thought of a possible liaison with the "young professor" that inspires in her memories of the younger Leopold trying to look like Byron, and that *may* even draw the couple together again. Before the extended exposure in "Penelope," we see Molly only briefly as Calypso, but her presence is felt everywhere Bloom goes. We get to know her as Bloom knows her and as others think they know her. For Bloom she is all, the omphalos about which he turns anxiously, the womb to which he returns, and the genetrix of his unborn son. Stephen, on the other hand, yearns for her as the Oedipal mate who will help fill the void left by his mother's death, complete his manhood, and perhaps mend his breeches before turning him out into the world. Curiously, it is this sort of relationship he rejects in "Ithaca," as Molly realizes through her monologue in "Penelope."

> I wonder why he wouldnt stay the night . . . he could easy have slept in there on the sofa in the other room I suppose he was as shy as a boy he being so young hardly 20 of me in the next room hed have heard me on the chamber arrah what harm . . . Id have to introduce myself not knowing me from Adam very funny wouldnt it Im his wife . . . itd be great fun supposing he stayed with us why not theres the room upstairs . . . Id love to have a long talk with an intelligent well-educated person Id have to get a nice pair of red slippers like those Turks with the fez used to sell or yellow and a nice semi-transparent morning gown that I badly want or a peachblossom dressing jacket like the one long ago in Walpoles only 8/6 or 18/6 Ill just give him one more chance . . . (778–80)

A circle would seem to have been closed by the last sentence, which reverts from Stephen to Bloom after Molly has united Stephen's dream of the East and Bloom's vision of her in Eastern dress. The offer of melons ("melons he held to my face . . . Come. Red carpet spread." (47)) has been refused "promptly, inexplicably, with amicability" (697) by Stephen but accepted by Bloom in Stephen's place, fulfilling both men, settling nothing, preparing the way for the sun to rise in the East. So much progress has been made.

Though apparently the least inhibited of them all, despite her appetites and bold talk, Molly has a rigid moral system. Joyce is playing here with the relationship of innocence to guilt, flesh to spirit, and sterility to fertility in the person of Calpe's daughter Marion, who may be as natural but is certainly not as free as the lady saluted by Mercurial Malachi at breakfast:

> —*For old Mary Ann*
> *She doesn't care a damn,*
> *But, hising up her petticoats* . . . (13)

It is worth noting that she spends more time justifying her fall in terms of Bloom's failures than she does reminiscing about her sexual adventures, that Boylan and Bloom are paired in her mind as sexual objects, that she is shocked by her own coarse language and seems to prefer euphemisms, and that she prefers Bloom in the end and makes a remarkably good case for her preference. Subject though she is to lunar influences (see the menstruation which takes her in the middle of her monologue), she represents the stable goal of male striving as well as the impulse that generates it. With logic, Joyce's schema identifies her with earth or substance and sees the web of words she spins (or the web of her attraction) as motion, for Stephen sees "movement" through Aristotle's definition as the "actuality of the possible as possible," (25) and Molly is the image of the word actualized as flesh. In *Finnegans Wake* the metaphor is expanded. Anna Livia Plurabelle, the primal Mother, is at once the destroyer, the prolonger and the protector of her all-Father husband Humphrey Chimpden Earwicker, supporter of the material universe. As daughter, Issy-Isolde, she tempts and betrays her father-husband Mark of Cornwall. As wife, she bears him 101 children. As the old hag, Kate the slop, she keens over him, buries him, and distributes his substance to his children. As defender and muse, she dictates the book or letter of life to her writer son, Shem the pen, a later version of the starveling Stephen, just as the boisterous Shaun the post, who delivers the letter, is a later version of Buck Mulligan (among others).

❦ III ❧

TWO CHARACTERS
AND A CITY-SCAPE

I

If, under Joyce's microscope, Bloom personifies everyman as outsider, his position is not unmotivated. Incapable of servicing Molly,
and essentially estranged from his daughter as love object, too self-
deprecating and insufficiently imaginative to "succeed" but too
abstemious and industrious to fail totally, too obviously alien and
cosmopolitan to be accepted by the Irish provincials and too Irish
not to be concerned, he is doomed to a perpetual search for the
center, which for him means balance. Seen from another angle, in a
society peopled by eccentrics, the outrageously moderate Bloom must
seem peculiar. Unlike Stephen, the rebel who consciously courts
rejection, Bloom must tread warily in the face of rejection. He
tempts no gods, risks no thunderous retribution, accepts his lot and
returns good for evil. Though the memory of his father's suicide
darkens his day and he contacts madness through Mr. Breen, he
risks neither. His main concern is to hang on to the social norm, to
confirm his position as father, husband, citizen, in a world that
repulses his advances on all fronts. He is out of phase with his
society and antiheroic in his adjustment, but he is without pride or
cynicism or pretense. Gross pragmatism, while occasionally a source
of wisdom, more often leads him clownishly to overvalue trifles that
Stephen just as absurdly ignores. His treatment of the cake of soap,
the flower, the card, his preoccupation with numbers, food, manners, and facts tend to make Bloom himself an object among objects
and prepare us for his eventual reduction to a catalogue of particulars in "Ithaca."

We watch through the daylight hours Bloom's growing preoccupation with a little knot of closely-related and virtually universal
concerns, which, during the evening hours, he faces on an instinc-
tual level. But if on this day the meaning of the key to his house

is made manifest to him, his worries make few visible ripples on the calm surface. Faced with Molly's infidelity and possible desertion, Milly's coming of age, and his failure to produce a son; haunted by the memory of his father and his own lack of a tradition in tradition-bound Ireland, he finds relief in exceptional social and mental activity. Individually, given their history and Bloom's disposition, none of these concerns is particularly grave. Coalescing under the heading "function," they demand some sort of resolution, for they constitute the everyman's reason for being. But given his peculiar relationship to Molly and the world, Bloom can do nothing about them. In the end, action takes the form of passive resignation or adjustment, the acceptance of the inevitable as inevitable. Bloom has come as close as he can to self-discovery and to the restoration of his manhood, and in the process he has incriminated and cleansed each of us of a variety of lusts and anguishes.

Though we find ourselves agreeing with Bloom's judgments, identifying with his foibles, understanding his errors, siding with him against adversaries, and preferring him over his peers, we are never allowed to forget his comic identity, to lose perspective or distance. His frustrations, conflicts, aspirations, inadequacies, fears and joys are always comic on a relative scale, just as his actions are often rendered funny by the reactions of others to them. When, among the outhouse fumes, he pictures himself a writer of pulp fiction and when he wipes himself with his model's story; when, busily researching for the Keyes advertisement, he mixes with the learned in the library; when, intent on seeing a woman's silk-stockinged calf, he is frustrated by a passing tram; when, against the citizen's monumental chauvinism and terrible envy, he preaches fair play and Christian love to the gentiles in Barney Kiernan's pub; when, in short, he pursues an infinitude of unworthy ends and brushes off innumerable slights and injuries, he plays the endearing fool in our eyes.

Perhaps the secret of Bloom's success lies in the fact that many of the shocks he deals to our sensibility are shocks of recognition light enough for us to endure and that the blows he receives bruise but do not break his spirit. Our introduction to the sensual man, coming as it does after our initiation into Stephen's perturbed and rarefied intellect is more like a warm bath than a cold shower. It may take a while for us to recognize ourselves in the kidney-eater who sees the cat's "lithe black form," and "the gloss of her sleek hide" and then pointedly notes "the white button under the butt of her tail." But after the metaphor-ridden thoughtstream of Stephen, Bloom's commonsense cat's-eye view of himself as a giant is endearing: "Wonder what I look like to her. Height of a tower? No, she can jump me." (55) Muffing an opportunity to assert his superiority, he has reduced himself to human size and proclaimed his vulnerability. Never straining for the right word, the precise thought, Bloom coasts along seeing only what is there and telling himself, never others, what he sees (as opposed to what he thinks). By contrast Joyce has made Stephen uncharitable and unapproachable, though admirable—the consummate ironist.

Unlike the traditional butt of comic or farcical laughter, Bloom has been turned into a surrogate perceiver and reactor for the unwary reader. In this he is very different too from the traditional first person narrator or even the modern unreliable narrator, both of whom set out to win our applause. To the extent that he comes to us through his stream of consciousness, he comes as one unaware of our presence and unprepared to make a play for sympathy. (It is appropriate that when Bloom makes a public bid for sympathy in "Cyclops," "Oxen of the Sun" or "Eumaeus," his companions respond negatively.) Perhaps Joyce has succeeded in making him seem a "good" man, for the expression in unguarded moments of his true and valid motives combined with his generous spirit, his freedom from cant, and his sharply focussed humorous view of life endear him to us as the habits of a canting Conmee and a crass Kernan in "Wandering Rocks" do not. Repeatedly, we share his unexpressed pain and distress and experience without sentimentality what relief is possible for him. We may even feel for him, what he cannot feel for himself, a painful embarrassment over his pleasures and tastes or a vague sadness over his failure to see his weakness vis-à-vis Stephen or to appreciate his strength in relation to Molly. Beyond all of this is our sense that Bloom is bigger than life, that he has been deliberately overdrawn as a monster of normality. The result is comedy, yes, but a comedy generously sprinkled with pathos which, like so much that is modern, turns back on the reader almost as much as it does on the weak, blind, foolish or stunted protagonist.

The fact that we know more about Bloom as a sentient human being than we do about any other literary hero does not set him apart. Quite the contrary, it underlines his role as the unexceptional man, l'homme moyen sensuel in Montaigne's famous phrase, a figure who experiences but does not capitulate to exceptional desires, who takes life as it comes, who expresses to himself what he prudently leaves unsaid, and represses what he fears to admit or face, a man who is neither brave nor cowardly. But every man is in some way separate from the crowd and Bloom is doubly distinguished, being not only a potential cuckold but a Jew in Dublin. A norm for the

world—the city man—he is nevertheless a fringe figure and an outsider in his own city if not in his own eyes. Joyce makes good use of
this condition, which gives Bloom enough distance from his fellows
to make him a perfect commentator on their foibles but leaves him
Irish enough and mature enough to show understanding and sympathy. Like Stephen's Shakespeare, he is more than just another
husband in what the unmarried John Eglinton calls a "French
triangle," just as he is more than that cliché of Jewish humor, the
Jew who takes it from all comers—a cultural Pierrot. For one thing
he is an accomplice in his fate as well as a victim, for another he has
not given up hope or resorted to acts of comic desperation. He is
also one who suffers for his indecision, a trait he shares with Stephen,
but, unlike Stephen and like the majority of men, he is not suffi-
ciently aware of himself to understand the nature of the decisions he
could make or to question the psychological motivation for his
errors.

Using Kierkegaard's categories, Arnold Goldman[1] has perceptively
defined Stephen in terms of his attitude as the "ironic" man and
Bloom as the "comic" man. An example might help clarify this distinction. Bloom with humorous pathos accepts the death of a casual
friend, saying "Poor Dignam," and with distanced anguish says "Poor
Papa" about his father, old and alone, deserted in the West of Ireland and sad enough to take a poisonous overdose of medicine.
Stephen, haunted too by his personal ghost, is clearly incapable of
saying with genuine or distanced sympathy, "poor mother," and
instead is forced to avenge her death on his own spirit while defend-
ing himself against the charge of matricide like a Fury-ridden Orestes.
The one man in his weakness recognizes the world in which he has
no power, the other in his strength sees the world as within himself,
and himself as responsible. Neither position is completely adequate,
but Stephen's is intolerable if not tragic while Bloom's is simply
undistinguished. Accordingly, still certain of his potential but emas-
culated by the ghost of his own inadequacy and feeling cheated of
his spiritual patrimony, Stephen wanders about "reading the book
of himself." Despair and guilt have left him almost as unsure of his
artistic vocation as he once was of his priestly one. However, if
Bloom's assurance is the product of ignorance and limited capacities,
Stephen's confusion is the confusion of brilliance and too much
knowledge. Discontented with and frustrated by the ideals toward
which his art and learning point, but unable to accept the world,
which could save him, he has turned to the Devil and become Mulligan's man. During his day he walks painfully in the Buck's cast-off
boots, testing the alternatives which his talents leave open to him:

teaching, journalism, scholarship, singing, living by his wits. Since he sees only desolation in his future and unpaid debts in his past, he is incapable of accepting or rejecting these temptations. It is his best qualities, his honesty and pride, that make him a bitter brooder and ascetic rather than a carefree hedonist like Mulligan or an amoral sponge like Lynch. As a result, he is what the Buck calls an "impossible person" (9), whose cynicism and irony are a negative faith which alone saves him from maudlin despair. The grotesque mock-heroic climax of "Circe" seems inevitable. The appropriate ironic response to a reasoned failure to take a stand is mindless action. He must be reduced and freed of his rational self so that he can make the gestures of rejection that will symbolically recapitulate the conclusion of the *Portrait,* obliterate what followed that false start, and restore him to youth and sanity. It matters and it does not matter that these gestures are no more than drunken maunderings, a pantomime of action, that he himself is unconsciously wearing at that moment the mask not of the artist-hero but of the pathetic clown, and that he neither breaks the light of the world nor holds his own in an argument against force. (Christ after all faced a similar failure and Hamlet achieved his goal only by inadvertence.) The climax of "Circe" approximates a tragic denouement, a moment of truth, a purging that should be followed at least in the mind of the reader by a theophany or elevation, suggested both by Bloom's vision of Rudy and by their shaky rapport in "Eumaeus" and "Ithaca," and confirmed in "Penelope." But Joyce's tragedy is in a minor key, jocular tragedy not to be taken *too* lightly, and what Stephen needs is not the father Mulligan says he seeks or the motherly woman he misses, but self assurance, a sense of humor, and objectivity, qualities possessed by Bloom in good measure.

Bloom and Stephen by nature and/or nurture exiles and opposites, are emotional father and son, but each needs the other in himself far more than in the flesh. It is with the younger Bloom, revitalized by her meditations on Stephen, that Molly may resume her relations. It is with his own mature self engaged by the world that Stephen may hopefully identify. Through concern for himself (a self he has habitually neglected), Bloom has obliged Molly to reconsider her rejection of him. After his experiment with sound in "Proteus," Stephen opens his eyes to find the world "there all the time without" him but then immediately translates the temporal into the eternal, adding "and ever shall be, world without end." (37) What Stephen needs is an awareness of the here and now. On the pragmatic level, though exile is a permanent and necessary condition for Stephen as artist and Bloom as Jew in Ireland, each can modify his adjustment. Bloom can live within the society into which he was born; accommodating himself to a split world-view and facing up to past failures, he can resume an ambiguous marital arrangement in a position of strength. Stephen can decide either to exist in a Dublin all of whose many facets are personally repugnant and obnoxious to his still distant goals as artist, or he can reject his guilt and allegiances along with offers of an easier life and, with his eyes open this time, make an unromantic second flight. Both must adjust in terms of Ireland (and Dublin), which becomes a middle term, a comitragic country that produces heroes and betrayers in equal numbers and a superabundance of dreamers and clowns.

II

Among Joyce's most astonishing feats is his vital and engaging portrait of Dublin as a modern commercial and cultural capital, ironically analogous to all cities in all ages. Dublin is a backdrop for action, a projection of Joyce's major protagonists, and a persona, which, like Stephen and Bloom, experiences a full day and night of life and exposes many facets of its personality. Though Stephen and Bloom are respectively a temperamental and a social outcast, and though they function within opposite sectors of the community, neither man occupies an extreme position in relation to a society that welcomes the one and barely tolerates the other. We see them reacting to and experiencing the essential life of a community which shades off from their positions towards fringes which are barely glimpsed. Still, between them, they survey and expose the worlds of commerce, journalism, education, music, and literature. With them we visit a school, the library, a newspaper office, the cemetery, a hospital, a whore house; we walk the streets and beaches, number the shops, inspect the monuments, watch (but don't ride) the trams, sample food and drink, and engage in conversations relevant to the concerns of the day. They take us from birth to death, from the church to the pub, from the bachelor's quarters to the home, from the pleasures and preoccupations of students and young dilettantes to those of the mature and settled if slightly seedy citizens. Joyce's pragmatic vision of Dublin is designed to put everything in its proper place. He is careful not to locate the center of the city, its heart, but he is also careful to put more emphasis on Bloom's world, on the world of normal social intercourse and popular culture epitomized on the positive side by Simon Dedalus and on the negative by the narrator of "Cyclops."

Stephen's father stands out as one of Joyce's great creations from life, a remarkably complete man given to us through his words and actions in four contexts and through the disparate responses of the major protagonists. A wastrel but not a scamp or a cheat, a wit but not devoid of sympathy, a gifted singer and popular social figure too lazy and dissolute to capitalize on his gifts, a potential womanizer who is no *roué*, a man at once selfish and self-pitying but one also capable of the gracious manner and full of the sap of life, a poor father who meditates bitterly on the company his son keeps but lets his family go hungry while he escapes through talk and drink, a bad husband who sentimentally mourns the wife he worked to death, Simon is, more than any other character, an embodiment of the graces and vices of Dublin. It is appropriate that, though he and Bloom have little real common ground, Simon occupies a central position in Bloom's world and that through him Stephen's and Bloom's social universes are momentarily joined. The relationship is confirmed along with Simon's character by Molly, whose epigrammatic characterizations are extraordinarily apt:

> . . . such a criticiser with his glasses up with his tall hat on him at the cricket match and a great big hole in his sock one thing laughing at the other and his son that got all those prizes for whatever . . . imagine [Poldy] climbing over the railings if anybody saw him that knew us wonder he didnt tear a big hole in his grand funeral trousers. . . . (768)

If we place Simon and his mildly genteel and gently improvident cronies in the center of Joyce's Dublin, the rest of the portrait follows logically but not mechanically. With the cool eye of an insider and the terse expression of a born raconteur, the thirsty dun of "Cyclops" gives us a whole range of lower middle class life and what is perhaps an unfair sampling of the revolutionary mentality. Other intersecting worlds are represented by other methods. Father Conmee, the former rector of Clongowes Wood school, one of Stephen's earlier fathers, and one of Joyce's sharpest satirical tools, supplements the glimpses of Dublin's spiritual life we get through Bloom in "Lestrygonians" and Gerty MacDowell in "Nausikaa." Gerty, who gives us the world of Irish single girls which she shares with Milly Bloom and the sirens in the Ormond bar, is in her turn supplemented by Molly in her reminiscences. Small boys are represented by Master Patrick Aloysius Dignam, a pale reflection of Stephen's Catholic childhood, who supplements the scene at Deasy's school and Stephen's own recollections.

Joyce's researches into the practical details of Dublin life, his

fidelity to the data in Thom's Dublin Directory, have become pro-
verbial, so much so that critics have made capital of his occasional
lapses.[2] In searching to convey the distinctive nature of the city
enshrined in his memory, he outdid himself and earlier realists. It is
almost a tribute to his success that a disturbed Dubliner once said
to me, "but you know he hasn't shown the real Dublin." It is obvious
that he hasn't shown the Dublin any one man would accept as his
city, anymore than he has in Bloom portrayed a man with whom
we can completely identify. But he has created a city that grows on
us and exceeds itself. Any Dubliner can point to places, types, or
customs slighted, but no one can deny the vitality of this canvas that
shades off from the center toward the excesses of poverty and wealth,
madness and death, gives us the contrasting public and private
worlds, and lets the day fade into the night. But the Dublin that we
have is a Dublin that we make, assembling the pieces in whatever
order suits us, in a manner that echoes Joyce's method in "Wandering Rocks," where the juxtaposed vignettes are cemented by the
interjection of parallel events.

As a town Dublin takes life as much from its role in the day of
Stephen, Bloom, and Molly as from thousands of trivial but vivid
details that constitute its substance, but it is not only a projection
of their experience of it, it is also a projection of their experience
of themselves. Each character, no matter how vivid he is in his own
right, exists in terms of Bloom and Stephen, and some characters,
while fulfilling minor roles in the book, exist most emphatically as
aspects of what these two wanderers are and projections of what they
might be. The technique is not a new one. We find variations on it
in Tolstoi, who sets up elaborate foils complete with antithetical contexts; in Balzac, who permits the "minor" characters of *Père Goriot*
to pump life into his hero Rastignac; in Flaubert's *Sentimental Education,* where the life Frédéric Moreau only samples is lived in
detail by a gallery of acquaintances almost as large as the cast of
Ulysses; and in chapter 5 of the *Portrait,* where each of Stephen's
friends represents both an aspect of the Ireland he will leave and
an indication of a direction he might otherwise follow. Thanks
partly to the dramatic method which allows Joyce to present characters without explicit commentary, we have in *Ulysses* an astonishing
range of vivid individuals among the minor figures. These latter
shade off almost imperceptibly from the vigorously presented Mulligan, to the shadowy loners, lunatics, and ghosts who seem to define
the limits of the knowable world, but who embody during the daylight hours the norms of the night and the repressed impulses of
normal people. At one extreme we have our anti-Stephens or our

anti-Blooms, at the other we have creatures turning into symbols, contributing to theme or merging with the landscape: Mrs. M'Guinness the plump pawnbroker and her Italianate namesake Denis J. Maginni, bald-deaf Pat the waiter, an old milk woman, a pugnosed tram driver, an affectionate policeman, lackeys, and even animals. Each of these lesser figures is distinguished by a single act or attribute, or epiphanized by Joyce's quick pen as in the following two portraits from "Hades":

> Mourners came out through the gates: woman and a girl. Leanjawed harpy, hard woman at a bargain, her bonnet awry. Girl's face stained with dirt and tears, holding the woman's arm looking up at her for a sign to cry. Fish's face, bloodless and livid.

> Coffin now . . . Horse looking round at it with his plume skeowways. Dull eye: collar tight on his neck, pressing on a bloodvessel or something. (101)[3]

Little more is seen of some minor characters who serve as foils for Stephen and Bloom. Still we have a sense of the individuality of Reuben J. Dodd (an embodiment of the avaricious Jew and the bad father, an object of hatred), Denis Breen (a projection of madness, a failed man, and an object of ridicule) or Mr. Purefoy (the prim Protestant progenitor and proper lower middle class Dubliner, who knows how to keep his wife faithful). Breen, whose name contains the same number of vowels and consonants as Bloom's, is emphatically associated with him as a "Half and half . . . that's neither fish nor flesh" in "Cyclops." (321) Breen spends his day wandering the streets of Dublin in a vain attempt to redress a grievance against the sender of an anonymous postcard containing nothing but the letters "U.p." Like Dodd and Purefoy, he never occupies the foreground and like them he is identifiable as a Pantaloon, the *Commedia dell' Arte* Merchant of Venice: "And begob what was it only that bloody old pantaloon Denis Breen in his bath slippers with two bloody big books tucked under his oxter . . ." (298) Joyce is of course playing with and against a stereotype which figures also in Stephen's discussion of Shakespeare and is inevitably identified with Bloom as cuckold, Jew, and dupe. The symbolic and analogical identities do not, however, rob Breen of verisimilitude. This pathetic little lunatic is seen from at least four angles. As husband, rival, citizen, and fixated madman, he takes life from his surroundings and from what we see of his life through the keyhole: "Cruelty to animals so it is," the narrator of "Cyclops" reflects in response to Bloom's plea for sympathy for Josie Breen,

to let that bloody povertystricken Breen out on grass with his beard
out tripping him, bringing down the rain. And she with her nose
cockahoop after she married him because a cousin of his old fellow's
was a pew opener to the pope. Picture of him on the wall with his
smashall sweeney's moustaches. (321)

Stephen, who feels more threatened by madness than Bloom, finds
his mad surrogate in the "constant reader" Cashell Boyle O'Connor
Fitzmaurice Tisdall Farrell, the dwarfish scion of an exhausted line,
who "parafes his polysyllables" in "Scylla." Following as it does the
Shakespeare discussion, during which Stephen forces himself into
Hamlet's boots, Farrell's appearance is ominous: "Item: was Hamlet
mad?" Stephen asks himself. (215) It is important that during "Lestrygonians," where Josie compares him to Breen, Bloom sees Farrell
walking "outside the lampposts" wearing a "tiny hat" that "gripped
his head" like a "skullpiece." (159)

By dint of juxtapositions and thematic or verbal echoes, Joyce
manages to link such disparate integers as the younger Dodd (the
suicidal son rejected by Simon in Bloom's presence), the "blind
stripling" (a cane-carrying "absentminded beggar," who leaves his
tuning fork at the Ormond and accidentally bumps into an enraged
Farrell), and Farrell himself. The network of relationships need not
stop there. Any reader can find legitimate ways of linking characters
contributing to the various themes of the book, which in turn are
generally linked to the major protagonists' main preoccupations.
We have among other things groups of ghosts, of suicides or drown-
ings, of moneylenders, of clowns and fools, of spoiled priests, and of
inadequate servants; and none of these groups needs to be validated
by the fascinating but tenuous analogical systems to which they all
inevitably contribute. Other minor characters represent not alternate trades or traits but alternate routes for Bloom or Stephen: the
panhandler Corley (one of the "Two Galants" in Dubliners), who
importunes Stephen in "Eumaeus," the Frenchified exile, Patrice
Egan, whose character is developed at length in "Proteus," and the
gentle, effeminate esthete and toady, Mr. Best, who featly foots it
through the library. Such relationships, and there are many more,
help identify the protagonists in terms of Dublin and the shifting
scene. They also emphasize those qualities or preoccupations of
which they are extreme examples, setting Stephen and Bloom (and
Molly, who must be related to other women) in a more normal light.
For all their individuality and despite the facts that make them
exiles in the community, Stephen, Bloom, and Molly are very Irish
in quirky Dublin, where every third individual is an eccentric
though only the exceptional few make capital of their quirks.

III

Chief among these exceptions are Mulligan and Boylan, "sunny" Buck and solar Blazes, a looking-glass couple of sufficient stature to function as opposite equivalents and rivals of the somber and lunar Stephen and Bloom. We may suspect that Boylan is Mulligan reduced to the crudest terms, the flashy vulgarian as opposed to the vulgar dandy; for Mulligan, like Wilde, is something of a "pretender" or poseur. Like Stephen he seems to wear a mask which we can pierce only occasionally, as when he shows anxiety over Stephen's grievance in "Telemachus": "A light wind passed his brow, fanning softly his fair uncombed hair and stirring silver points of anxiety in his eyes." (8) At such moments we understand Stephen's attachment to him or to the hidden frailty revealed in this case through a trick of light. There is also strength and generosity, vigour, and wit. Mulligan has saved a man from drowning. He will give willingly, though ostentatiously, of his substance and as willingly accept. He can praise as well as scorn. These are all qualities admired and resented by Stephen, whose courage and generosity are muted by terror and insecurity and whose pride forces him to accept the gift while rejecting the giver.

Buck takes his nickname from an eighteenth century Dublin rake, but the name also suggests the goat of lechery and whimsy, a joyous but unstable and treacherous figure whose very gestures he imitates in "Telemachus": "He capered before them . . . fluttering his winglike hands, leaping nimbly." (19) Joyce spares no pains to make him appealing (in complete contrast to the gloomy and self-obsessed Stephen), gratuitously but delightfully witty and obscene, cultivated but not pedantic, full of himself but insouciant in his "primrose waistcoat." When he enters even the most dismal room, we experience the lift given when sunlight pierces the clouds. He is indeed "tripping and sunny" with his "yellow dressinggown," his goldpointed white teeth (Stephen's are rotten), his airy manner, and his enviable vocabulary of amusing gestures. Mulligan practices effortlessly, if frivolously, the art which Stephen, going J. K. Huysmans and the symbolists one better, preaches in "Circe": "So that gesture, not music, not odours, would be a universal language, the gift of tongues rendering visible not the lay sense but the first entelechy, the structural rhythm." (432) Buck also practices with gracious and disconcerting facility the arts of poetry and rhetoric, while enjoying financial independence and the prospect of a secure future as a doctor. Despite himself, Stephen sees in him an enviable model. Throughout the day, we see him desperately but mistakenly trying to imitate the Buck's contagious charm, to assume his mask as earlier he has assumed others: "Proudly walking," he recalls in "Proteus." "Whom were you trying to walk like? Forget: a dispossessed." (41) As a performer Stephen predictably fails. His is the "darkness shining in brightness" (48) that brightness fails to comprehend. His wit is ironic, biting, pointed, and never gratuitous—the scholastic's "lancet." (7) He seems automatically, though not without bitterness, to assume the role of victim which he shares with Bloom, just as Mulligan shares with Boylan the role of sunny conqueror. Formerly, he has welcomed Cranly as a secular confessor; now he accepts his subservience to Buck as an emblem of shame and a symbol of failure. It is characteristic that Mulligan is unaware of this and insensitive to his friend's feelings, but so polished is his mask of mindless and carefree folly, that he has earned the fool's privileges and his license goes unpunished.

Buck appears to have seduced the very muse that sent Stephen winging to Paris. During his day Stephen manages to produce only a miserable quatrain written on a scrap of paper torn from Deasy's hoof and mouth letter:

> On swift sail flaming
> From storm and south
> He comes, pale vampire,
> Mouth to my mouth. (132)

(It is characteristic of Joyce's irony that he identifies the paper used by Stephen with the prize story used by the aspiring pulp fiction writer, Bloom, in his privy.) Buck on the other hand turns out clever, off-color spoofs effortlessly and broadcasts them to the amused mob. He is what Dublin would call an "artist," meaning the accomplished jokester.[4] There is however another side to his character: his literary and perhaps personal decadence. From the start he is identified with the art and person of Oscar Wilde[5] as opposed to the lushly erotic and masochistic Swinburne, whom he quotes but whom Joyce pairs with Stephen. Mulligan, the faddist and exhibitionist, a man who like Wilde would be apt to make his life his art, is the worst possible exemplar and the most dangerous rival for one who feels he must elaborate out of himself painfully, in the manner of Shem the pen,[6] and who has dedicated himself to "silence, exile, and cunning." [7] The full extent of the danger is illustrated by the brief scene in "Wandering Rocks" where the erstwhile friend and supporter tells Haines of Stephen's absurd plan to "write something in ten years."

(249) Friendship with Mulligan, were there any stability in it, might lead to acceptance in Ireland, but it constitutes in fact an inhibition to freedom. Buck becomes in the course of this book the prime symbol of the forces trying to shape Stephen into what he cannot be, forces toward which Stephen feels dangerously drawn: "Staunch friend, a brother soul: Wilde's love that dare not speak its name. He now will leave me. And the blame? As I am. As I am. All or not at all." (49) The reference to "Wilde's love," or homosexuality, points up a final aspect of the relationship, which Stephen would reject as he has formerly rejected Cranly, an aspect that colors both the Shakespeare argument and Stephen's contact with Bloom.

Unlike Stephen, who seems to choose his torments, Bloom is the passive victim of his weaknesses. Unlike Mulligan, who is much less "bad" than his words suggest, Boylan is the physical usurper, the vulgar seducer whose virility Bloom envies and fears. It is comically appropriate that after he has played the seducer in a minor key to Gerty, Bloom finds himself identifying masochistically with the gaudily dressed conqueror: "Us too: the tie he wore, his lovely socks and turnedup trousers. He wore a pair of gaiters the night that first we met. His lovely shirt was shining beneath his what? of jet." (369) As a reflection on Bloom's own weakness, the lover's actions are in a sense controlled by the husband's inaction. He is the classic fancyman, the gay seducer of the wives of negligent husbands, the hero of countless bedroom farces, the idol of the lesser pub characters and the shopgirls. But he is more: a caricature of the type, cruder, bolder, dumber, a Dublin "billsticker." An operator, a speculator who trades on Dublin's foibles, who even plays at being an impresario, Boylan is still a brightly colored, jaunty, jingling Harlequin. Joyce presents him obliquely through the eyes and reactions of characters who hardly know him, as a self-centered fellow, a loner who passes frequently but seldom stops to chat. He speaks in fact a bare handful of words and remains a figment of the public imagination. Bloom draws him out of the pornographic books he reads and confuses him with a variety of subliterary types. Even Molly can depict only the sexual animal, speaking with mixed admiration and distaste of his performance and his lapses into grossness and rage. But there is no need to complete the stereotype which stands in opposition to the most developed character in literature and paradoxically draws life from the ultrasophisticated Mulligan, Bloom's rival for the affections of Stephen. The two figures from opposite cultural milieux help like Stephen and Bloom to describe the centers of which they are extreme examples. Thus the bounder who knows how to use the commercial, the sporting and the musical centers, which accept him in full awareness of the liberties he takes, is as much a measure of these aspects of Dublin as Mulligan is of the intellectual, professional, and artistic worlds whose measurements he takes. Joyce has neatly circumscribed his city with his four compass points projected against a subtly realized physical and spiritual map.

⋙ IV ⋘

ADJUNCTS TO MEANING

I

We cannot ignore the fact that Joyce modeled *Ulysses* after *The Odyssey*. He made this clear when he named his book and inescapable when he gave Herbert Gorman his schema and encouraged Stuart Gilbert to explore the analogy in detail. But like Vergil before him, he has taken enormous liberties with his model, while, unlike Vergil, he has neither created a second Ulysses nor set Homer's hero up as the embodiment of unalloyed virtue. Though we may pass over many of the details of the schema, which points up Joyce's preoccupation with universals (the human organism, the components of life, the hours and phases of a day, the arts of man, etc.), we must accept and deal with the analogical implications latent in the homeric title, episodes, and characters; for to a degree they dictated the form of the book, and even now they clarify the nature of the heroes' quests and identities. Joyce chose Homer's hero as his model for Bloom because Ulysses was to his mind the most complete character in literature, a figure seen from many points of view, engaged in many activities, in terms of his many functions. Like Ulysses, Bloom is, according to Joyce, "a complete man" as well as a "good man," though not necessarily ideal.[1] The word "good," as suggestive as it is vague, doubtless applies also to the world Joyce surveys, if we are to take Molly Bloom's final "yes" in its fullest sense.

Ulysses' three subdivisions, the "Telemachia," the "Odyssey," and the "Nostos," (i.e., the return) correspond to the three main sections of *The Odyssey*. Joyce's first three chapters approximate Homer's account of how Telemachus, awakened to manhood by Athena, goes out into the world to test his powers and discover what can be learned about his father's whereabouts. The twelve chapters of the central section roughly parallel Homer's account of Ulysses' departure from Calypso, the nymph who has kept him prisoner of love, and his visit with the Phaeacians to whom he tells the tale of

51

his travels and misfortunes before they transport him back to Ithaca. In the "Nostos," Joyce's Ulysses reveals himself to his "son." Together they slaughter the suitors so that the hero may regain his kingdom, rejoin his faithful and long-suffering Penelope, and set out on his final quest.

At once delightfully literal and boldly free with his model, Joyce took joy in establishing ironic and interpretative analogies for even the least of Homer's details:

> I am now writing the Lestrygonians episode, which corresponds to the adventure of Ulysses with the cannibals. My hero is going to lunch. But there is a seduction motive in the Odyssey, the cannibal king's daughter. Seduction appears in my book as women's silk petticoats hanging in a shop window. The words through which I express the effect of it on my hungry hero are: "Perfume of embraces all him assailed. With hungered flesh obscurely, he mutely craved to adore." [2]

Other passages are more obviously and playfully homeric. Take for example the broadly cannibalistic reflection elicited by the array of food at Davy Byrne's "moral pub": "Ham and his descendants mustered and bred here. Potted meats. What is a home without Plumtree's potted meats? Incomplete . . . Under the obituary notices they stuck it . . . Dignam's potted meat."—and so on with gusto. The homeric allusions in passages like these may be overlooked by the reader upon whose consciousness they are working, but the whimsy and the joy underlying their invention will not. Since they do not correspond directly or exclusively to anything homeric, but only to Joyce's idiosyncratic reading of Homer from a modern perspective, they do not detract from the organic unity of the book.

Already by "Proteus," [3] Joyce's third chapter, we are aware that he has shaped his book less in terms of the analogy than of the situations of his major protagonists. Homer's poem recounts Telemachus' visit to Menelaus' palace where the aging hero tells the tale of his return from Troy, emphasizing his struggle with the sea god Proteus, who, once stilled, loses his power to change shape and must tell his conqueror how to escape from the island of Pharos. The god's nature impregnates Joyce's chapter where Stephen becomes the focal figure, a sort of combination of Menelaus on Pharos, Telemachus as his guest in Sparta, and by virtue of the uneasy flux of his mind, Proteus himself. Most of the original action is conveyed analogically, but everything is displaced in favor of Stephen's identity crisis, which is in itself a projection of the problem of a fatherless Telemachus searching for his function. (Actually Stephen is trying to shed Telemachus' duties in order to exercise those of the free spirit.) In the central chapters Joyce goes much further. The order of the episodes is rudely shifted. "Nausikaa" follows "Cyclops" rather than (as in Homer) "Calypso." While Ulysses tells the tale of his travels to the Phaeacians (his narrative taking up most of the central portion), Bloom confines himself to a three-line recapitulation in "Nausikaa": "Long day I've had. Martha, the bath, funeral, house of keys, museum with those goddesses, Dedalus' song. Then that bawler in Barney Kiernan's. Got my own back there." (380) Joyce's "Hades" follows his "Lestrygonians" rather than (again as in Homer) "Circe." "Wandering Rocks," missing from Homer's account, is inserted as a pivotal chapter. Stephen-Telemachus' voyage dovetails with Bloom-Ulysses' travels. The fantasia in Circe's den, which falls so early in Homer's version, closes the central section and provides the book with its major dramatic climax bodying forth an inferno more terrible than anything in "Hades." Joyce's innovations are even more obvious in the "Nostos," where Homer's unwieldy but suspense-and-action-packed return chapters are condensed into three virtually static episodes and the last word rises voluminous from the recumbent, unfaithful, and impatient Molly, the secret of whose jingling bed Bloom-Ulysses does not know.

Stuart Gilbert points out that Joyce had good reasons for choosing the half-piratical warrior chieftain as his parallel and a Jew as his protagonist.[4] Dublin's founding fathers were after all sea rovers too and the earliest invaders and colonists are thought to have come from Greece or Scythia. One of Joyce's sources, Victor Bérard's *Les Phéniciens et l'Odyssée,* insists that Homer derived his travel narrative from the tales spun by Phoenician traders, Semites like Bloom. Ireland is in many ways similar to Greece, though the situation of the Irish in our times resembles that of the Jews in Roman times. The justification may be elaborated much further, as indeed Joyce did in his rough notes, but of course Leopold Bloom is not Ulysses. He is rather the type of Ulysses, a latter-day exemplar isolated from wife and family by death and emotional distance. Neither is he heroic. He is hard put to cope even with the troubles of the little man in a modern, turbulent city. Stephen is not (like Telemachus) a fatherless Greek ephebe who sheds his fears when he sails out into the big world. Instead he is a gifted but rather confused and dreamy Irish youth, unwashed, uncourageous, with frustrated ambitions. Yet, like Telemachus, he must somehow be grounded in reality before he can hope to achieve anything. In each case the analogy is ironical and the irony cuts two ways to establish a fresh relationship and new attitudes toward the givens of both narratives. If Bloom is analogous to Ulysses, and we can point not only to their parallel adventures but to traits that they share, then Bloom is ennobled by the conjunction with the hero. But since he falls so far short in his nature and behavior and in the quality of his adventures, we must also see him as diminished by the relationship, a grotesque shadow of the heroic precursor. The two attitudes generated by Joyce's metaphor, though virtually opposite, do not negate each other. Instead, they set up a fruitful tension within our conception of the chapter and illuminate our hackneyed view of the heroic prototype.

As part of a hardening and polishing process, Homer's Athena sends the callow Telemachus to visit Nestor, the king of horse-rich Pylos, before she sends him to the warrior prince, Menelaus. Nestor is a gentle, pious, fatherly sort who will be tolerant of the boy's awkwardness. As it happens, Telemachus does astonishingly well, impresses the wise old man with his bearing and tact, and participates in a sacrifice before being sent on his way with good advice. In *Ulysses* the allusions to this event and the parallels are numerous and specific, and neither Nestor-Deasy's experience nor Stephen's callowness are in question. But Joyce's Telemachus is a teacher as well as a pupil, and though he listens patiently enough, he is embarrassed, and galled by the old man's preachments. It is ironic, given Stephen's antinationalist sentiments, that Deasy links him to the Fenians and, given his artistic credo, that he identifies him with journalism. It is more ironic that the old Orangeman's opinions provoke reactions that underline Stephen's failure to sever the ties that bind him to Ireland and Irish causes. Despite himself, Stephen cannot join the horse-fancying Orangeman in an attack on his own freely rejected church and party. His is still the not invalid Catholic position that the Protestant establishment has camped on the prostrate body of the majority. Unlike Telemachus, the Ithacan bumpkin, who is overawed by the splendor of the rich king's facilities, Stephen is unimpressed by Deasy's connections, his possessions and his "wisdom." Unlike the generous Nestor, Deasy is a provincial, free with advice but lacking in respect for Stephen's forefathers, and stingy with his money. Still Deasy is no more a simple caricature of Nestor than Stephen is of Telemachus. (After all, Homer's "tamer of horses" is of remarkably little help to his visitor, who must in the end rely on his own powers.) Both are freely adapted and ironically conceived projections whose relationships to the Greek originals are strikingly similar to Stephen's relationship to Bloom.

The freedom with which Joyce adapted his sources can be seen also in the expansion of a minor episode like the perilous voyage between the rock Scylla and the whirlpool Charybdis. Here he elaborated a splendid conceit, letting the spartan life in Stratford stand for the rock while the whirlpool is symbolized by Plato, syncretistic mysticism, and the profuse life of London. He presents John Eglinton (the dogmatic country boy, who champions Aristotle), and AE (the theosophical aesthete and platonist), as the poles between which Stephen hangs his argument, bending this way or that to mollify and please the opponents he wishes to woo. Inevitably Stephen is caught in both traps, from which Mulligan's wit unpleasantly extricates him. Bloom, who enters the library in time to see Stephen rent and submerged, is untouched by learning and reason. Like Ulysses, he passes through unscathed, though he is already drawn to Stephen as surrogate son (if not as a lost crew member). The danger has of course been ludicrously minimal. But Joyce was not content with this; he felt the need to expose Bloom further. Accordingly, he ended his chapter by having him sail through the library portals between the whirlpool of irony (Stephen) and the rock of mockery and malice (Mulligan), a genuine escape if a comic one.

II

The *Odyssey* analogies are the most carefully elaborated of Joyce's allusions, but the others, though less pronounced, are by no means gratuitous. Though there is no reason to maintain in so rich a context a constant awareness of subidentities which are only periodically underlined, we take pleasure in the sudden discovery of a subtly stated parallel and the consequent enlargement of the being of one of the protagonists and of the book's frame. Bloom-Ulysses-Shakespeare-Dante-Ahazuerus-St. Anthony-God-etcetera and Stephen-Telemachus-Hamlet-Shakespeare-Icarus-Daedalus-Faust-Wandering Aengus-Christ-etcetera do not exist as cluster characters but rather as single and singular personages sharing with their models certain distinguishing traits and oscillating between and among the possibilities thus suggested. There may be no hard and fast rule for the "identifications," but we note that frequently they come in antagonistic pairs, sometimes in unified groups of three (Telemachus, Ulysses, Penelope; Hamlet, Shakespeare, Ann Hathaway); often they attract a whole body of subsidiary relationships (see for example the way the Hamlet analogy invites us to identify Deasy with Polonius or Mulligan and Haines with Rosencrantz and Guildenstern).[5] At times they are actually part of the character's view of himself or others. Thus, in a Byronic mood, Stephen sees himself as the fallen

Lucifer or Icarus while under other auspices he identifies with a betrayed Christ or an accomplished Daedalus. The hints are there, the substructure has been carefully elaborated but, as we may recall, few noticed even the most obvious of the analogies until Stuart Gilbert published his study.

Though Joyce told Frank Budgen that Faust, as opposed to the many-sided Ulysses, is rootless, "no-aged" and incomplete,[6] Goethe's *Faust* was one of the earliest correlatives for *Ulysses*. As early as 1907, Joyce explained to his brother Stanislaus that his novel "would depict an Irish Faust, heroic and full of presumption." As Richard Ellmann remarks, he had probably begun to think of the book as autobiographical.[7] It is a critical commonplace that Joyce patterned "Circe" after the famous witches' sabbath or *Walpurgisnacht,* but it is not widely recognized that he used the analogy elsewhere. Yet, we do not need his comments to discover similarities between Faust and Stephen as romantic overreachers. Having devoted a lifetime to seeking union with the absolute through study and teaching, Faust discovers that he has earned only fatigue and disillusionment. In his tomblike study he turns to magic books, hoping to gain illegitimately what he could not achieve by legitimate (sanctified or scholastic) means. After his failure with the Earth Spirit, who rejects him as a half-man living only in his mind, he contemplates suicide before capitulating to Mephistopheles, who restores his youth and permits him to complete his identity. Stephen's case is both strikingly similar and remarkably different. Having cultivated only one side of his being and nourished himself on dead learning "coffined thoughts . . . in mummycases, embalmed in spice of words," (193) he too lives among shriveled hopes in a kind of cell (see the tower and his mind). He too acts the teacher unconvinced by his teaching, contemplates suicide, meditates on the purpose of life, recognizes but is frustrated by the need for change, and fears the fall from grace. Though we can understand his disillusionment, there is something absurd about Stephen's self-involvement, his love of abstruse lore, his inability to shed the chains of a religion to which he no longer feels committed, his perverse asceticism. It seems inappropriate for so young a man to be so crabbed and aged, so sober even when drunk, so intense. Yet these are all temporary Faustian traits which combine with a permanent Faustian inner energy and drive. For the rest, that merry devil Mulligan does his living for him, and provides a model and a goad he distrusts, fears, and envies.

The *Faust* themes coalesce towards the end of "Circe" where, reversing Faust's development, the witch's magic turns Stephen momentarily from a boy into an old man:[8] *"His features grow drawn and grey and old."* (582) The moment is particularly Faustian, following as it does the dance with a whore-witch and the vision of a *"green crab with malignant red eyes"* emanating from his mother, who doubles in this context as the innocent Gretchen whom Faust got with child. This is a conflation of details from several incidents. In *Faust* a red mouse emerges from the mouth of the naked young witch with whom the old-young man is dancing and Gretchen is seen as dead but still intact, a warning of her impending execution for infanticide. Faust's reaction is one of passionate sympathy and repentance for having left her to this fate. Stephen rebels, breaks from the memory in terror and disgust. His need is to rid himself of the "agenbite of inwit" (remorse of conscience) rather than to enlarge upon it.

A less dramatic and more typical example is Stephen's second appearance in "Wandering Rocks," where the context more than justifies references to the scholar-magician, whose frustration at the beginning of Goethe's play-book parallels the young man's claustrophobia. Here Stephen wanders aimlessly from a jeweler's window to a bookseller's cart where he contemplates an odd assortment of books and meets his sister Dilly. Superficially, there are no parallels for this action in *Faust*. (Stephen's graphic vision of death by drowning and his confession of guilt remind one more of *Hamlet*.) The lapidary's unburied treasure, however, recalls fallen angels and brings on visions of hellish terrors and Circean ("swinish") oriental delights. In the larger context it also suggests Mephisto's method of supplying Faust with wealth. Stephen becomes more specifically Faustian when he muses unhappily on his kinship with the gem-polishing jeweler, a creature from a lower world: "Grandfather ape gloating on a stolen hoard. And you who wrest old images from the burial earth! The brainsick words of sophists: Antisthenes. A lore of drugs." (242) Like Faust he is aware that his knowledge is corrupt, little better than the "base treasure of a bog" (29) he noticed in Deasy's office. At his next stop, the dusty bookcart with its load of dead learning, Stephen finds a book with magical spells by an abbot, Peter Salanka, whom he mockingly equates with his own favorite, Joachim de Flora. It is from this sort of text that Goethe's hero extracts the spells that raise the devil. The murmured spell (*"—Se el yilo nebrakada femininum!"* (242)) brings Dilly, whom Stephen pictures by the fire in a vignette that may recall the famous "Witches' Kitchen" scene: "It glowed as she crouched feeding the fire with broken boots." (243) This is the moment of Faust's magical transformation into a youth, during a scene which features, along with the witch and her sire, the witch's apes and the mirror in which

Faust sees the reflection of his ideal. Like her mother in "Circe,"
Dilly does double duty, suggesting both witch and Gretchen and
more. She also functions as his mirror: "My eyes they say she has.
Do others see me so? Quick, far and daring. Shadow of my mind."
Ironically, her eyes give him back no inspiration, no light, only
deep despair and the vision of her-him drowning in "Misery!
Misery!" (243)

Telemachus and Faust are among the exceptions to the rule that
Stephen supplies his own subidentities. Bloom's identities, in accordance with Joyce's more light-hearted conception of him, and
apart from the *Odyssey* framework, are generally evolved by others.
Stephen works out the motivation and condition of Shakespeare,
which we in our turn apply to Bloom's situation as a mastered and
cuckolded husband, and a father, whose dead son would now be
about eleven, the age when Hamnet Shakespeare died. Goaded by
Eglinton, Stephen goes so far as to find "Jewish" traits in the playwright, traits which Bloom ironically enough lacks. For the most
part, the plodding, tasteless Dublin Jew is Shakespeare in contra-
distinction to as well as in terms of Stephen's definition. Yet, when
Stephen concludes his argument with something resembling a creator's credo, we suddenly discover striking, pointed, and even plausible relationships between Shakespeare as artist-God, God the creator,
and Leopold Bloom, the former employee of a slaughter house and
the husband who implicitly offers his wife to others:

> . . . the lord of things as they are whom the most Roman of catholics
> call *dio boia,* hangman god, is doubtless all in all in all of us, ostler
> and butcher, and would be bawd and cuckold too but that in the econ-
> omy of heaven, foretold by Hamlet, there are no more marriages,
> glorified man, an androgynous angel, being a wife unto himself. (213)

In *Ulysses,* more emphatically than Stephen or any other character,
Bloom is the "lord of things as they are," not only in the sense that
he is supremely aware of pragmatic reality but also in Stephen's
Aristotelian sense that his soul or "form of forms" incorporates more
since it apprehends more of Dublin than any other soul in the book.
(In a jocular vein Bloom's masturbation fulfills the prediction in
the last phrase of the citation.)

Joyce scatters other identities for Bloom broadcast through the
novel. He lets Mulligan, for example, identify him with the Wandering Jew in "Scylla," and suggests, through Stephen in "Proteus,"
a Moses identity. He links Bloom to Elijah, whose return will an-
nounce the Last Judgment and the Second Coming, through the
throwaway he tosses into the river Liffey, through the concluding

commentary in "Cyclops," and through juxtaposition in the conclusion to "Oxen of the Sun." As a projection of Jehovah, Bloom
gathers up the fallen Stephen, a projection of the slain Christ, and
with the aid of death's representative Corny Kelleher protects him
from the watch so that he may escort him to the abode of bliss.
(Such parallels are confirmed, or rather reaffirmed, in the most
hilarious manner during "Circe," where Bloom takes on a whole
constellation of further but clearly spurious identities and even
becomes momentarily feminine.) One suspects that Bloom as law
giver and messiah would be far better than the citizen but little
better than his own hallucinated persona in "Circe," where he pro-
claims the "new Bloomusalem in the Nova Hibernia of the future"
(484) and announces his version of the Ten Commandments:

> Union of all, jew, moslem and gentile. Three acres and a cow for all
> children of nature. Saloon motor hearses. Compulsory manual labour
> for all. All parks open to the public day and night. Electric dish-
> scrubbers. Tuberculosis, lunacy, war and mendicancy must now cease.
> General amnesty, weekly carnival, and masked licence, bonuses for all,
> esperanto the universal brotherhood. No more patriotism of bar-
> spongers and dropsical impostors. Free money, free love and a free lay
> church in a free lay state. (489–90)

In mocking Bloom here, Joyce mocks as well the aspirations of Jews
and Irish alike, for both desire an impossible earthly kingdom. It is
not always clear how we should take these and other identifications,
but surely most of them are absurd and grotesque in ways that the
Odyssey and Shakespeare parallels are not. Possibly Joyce had set
out to undermine most emphatically the grave aspects of this book
which are associated with Stephen and his fate, by re-projecting his
other-worldly concerns in terms of a clownish emblem of humanity
whose virtues outweigh his faults but hardly merit such stiff-necked
seriousness. Stephen, as he is presented to us in *Ulysses*, is imbued
with the sort of fanaticism and dogmatism which characterized the
Jews in ancient times. Bloom, despite his inadequacies, is characteristically easy going, delighting in his humanity, and delighted by
the world and the flesh. For him the world of the spirit, "that other
world," is simply a typing error in a coy letter. (77)

In this connection we have an identification for Bloom that cor-
responds to the Faust identity for Stephen, namely with Flaubert's
ascetic hermit Saint Anthony. The hero of *La Tentation de St.
Antoine*[9] is a proper response to the romantic overreacher in *Faust*.
Both works have contributed (perhaps with some side glances at
Dante) to the form of Joyce's "Circe," which, like them, is written

as a play and which combines and blends their attributes. If in that chapter Stephen's experiences follow those of the peripatetic Faust whose comic devil (see Lynch in "Circe" and Mulligan elsewhere) is partly a projection of his psychic need, Bloom experiences the hallucinatory frenzy of an immobile Saint Antoine, whose visions reconstitute in a disorderly fashion his past and embody his repressed desires in like profusion. The worldly but curiously abstemious, isolated and naïve Bloom is ironically cast as the self-tormenting saint, who has rejected the world only to find it within his own nature. The unworldly and ascetic Stephen, who has been thrown in the middle of the action to which he has yet to adjust, is both appropriate and anomalous in the Faustian role of a scholar-hero who rejects explicitly the sort of life Stephen is leading between pubs, libraries, and student carouses.

The Shakespeare-Hamlet framework is appropriate to the themes of fatherhood, exile and estrangement, adultery, death, divinity, and creativity, which constitute the bulk of Joyce's thematic concerns. The Faust and Saint Antoine framework can accommodate a number of others. But since it is not stated as a theme but rather made to contribute directly to the form, and hence available like the *Odyssey* but lower on the scale of values, it functions principally as a means of corroborating the larger development of the day, paralleling the drift of Stephen and Bloom toward self-fulfillment and resignation. Just as Stephen and Bloom momentarily combine to make a complete man who might resemble Shakespeare and contribute to a Shakespearian trinity, the *Walpurgisnacht* in which Faust recognizes the depths to which he has sunk and Saint Antoine's night of tormenting self-discovery and disillusionment combine to create the drama of disclosure which inverts the daytime identities of Stephen and Bloom and permits them to achieve spiritual unity.

Clowns and clowning constitute yet another sort of mesh in Joyce's analogical net, one which joins the two principal character groups in a vital but distinctly conventional formal union and at the same time engages us in a new thematic and structural complex. The clown figure is introduced emphatically on page one with the prancing, prating, mocking Buck Mulligan, the jester of the Irish literary revival, a figure whose type conforms to the conventional pantomime and *Commedia dell' Arte* figure of mirth and mischief, Harlequin. Mulligan and Boylan constitute a pair; Bloom and Stephen, as their somber and ill-favored counterparts, each function as a projection of the sad clown, Pierrot. Molly, in obvious conjunction with the pastoral Gerty and possibly also with Stephen's fickle muse, is identifiable as Columbine. While Bloom and Boylan are clearly clowns by nature on the stage of life, Stephen and Mulligan consciously hide behind the mask created by literary predecessors. If Buck is the most polished performer, Bloom is the most versatile clown, and the most engaging. His apotheosis in "Circe," coming after we have discerned in chapter after chapter traces of the gently ridiculous, is a farrago of traditions and techniques disclosing the accomplished mime, the fool of many faces whose strength lies in his display of weakness. Unconsciously, he becomes the most conventional sort of performer, projecting in a number of guises mock mastery and endearing humiliation. By contrast Stephen, who has to his own mind played the jester while teaching, disputing or prating grave nonsense, becomes in "Circe" the frenetic puppet, a pathetic version of Mulligan (19), "with shrugged shoulders, finny hands outspread, a painted smile on his face" (569) before rushing madly to a mock-destruction reminiscent of the fate of so many post-Romantic Pierrots. It is consistent with Joyce's method that the farcical "Circe," where comic stereotypes are dominant, is the most serious of the book's chapters, the one that exposes and cleanses, for the moment at least, the deepest wounds. Here we are far nearer the truth of Stephen's dilemma than we are in either "Proteus," where Stephen is masked against himself, or "Scylla," where he is armed against others. Likewise Bloom, in acting out in sequence the most degrading roles, has reached a bottom from which he can only rise.

If we bear in mind their existence and are not distracted by their subtle glow, the analogies have many practical functions. Through them, the characters can complete not one but many actions, live many lives, resume history, achieve heroic or divine stature. They can be united metaphorically or be made to conform to the structures of various logical systems. Since these are no more than analogies, no such identification need in fact occur and the realistic "curve" is maintained. Through them also the logic of time and place is distorted and we achieve a sense of the universal as a component of a statement of particularity. This is not the case in Joyce's next book, which, in accordance with his practice, reverses the concerns of *Ulysses* and places the analogical identities first, letting us pierce through an awareness of the "omnibody" ("Here Comes Everybody") to a sense of the modest individual who is nobody in particular.

III

"Pooh!" says the Wilde-like dandy Mulligan, "We have grown out of Wilde and paradoxes. It is quite simple. He proves by algebra that Hamlet's grandson is Shakespeare's grandfather and that he himself is the ghost of his own father." (18) Joyce never goes quite this far, but he does base his book in paradox. This is probably inevitable in a book which combines a Platonic "symbolism" (a tendency to deal with man as a glass through which we glimpse a higher or at least more universal reality) with an Aristotelian "realism" (a tendency to treat existence as an opaque fact). One thinks of Joyce's favorite heretic, Giordano Bruno (1548–1600), the philosopher of Nola, who insisted that opposites are identical, that the greatest is equivalent to the least, the longest to the shortest, the coldest to the hottest, the finite to the infinite, and who, centuries before Leibnitz, generated out of apparent disharmony the real harmony of the world.[10] Whatever its merits as philosophy, this principle, which appropriately contradicts without completely invalidating the Aristotelian bases for the book, served Joyce well in *Ulysses,* where he pitted every aspect against not one but several opposite equivalents, and where unity is found through the vital instability of these relationships.

The bright cloudless day through which men wander blind to their needs and harried by their aspirations is seen in relation to the evening and night where they find enlightenment and discover themselves in their hidden nature. The un-Irish Bloom is equated with and set against the city which rejects him. Stephen is paradoxically identified with a man who is in every apparent sense his antitype. The analogical systems, each of which is based on paradoxical relationships, clash when they are juxtaposed. How do we go about identifying Ulysses' travels, the Passion of Christ, and Shakespeare's life? Structural elements are pitted against passages that set them in fresh ironic light. "Cyclops," with its discordant male voices, its medley of styles, its low narrator and comic Irish spirit and its concluding catastrophe, is echoed in "Oxen of the Sun" where the contrived wit of the carousers is recounted in grave and elevated styles and the whole crew is flushed out into the night along with Mina Purefoy's afterbirth. It is essential that we compare and even equate the two circumstances, though they too are extremes, being on the one hand the expression of wasted lives through spontaneous folk wit and on the other of youthful potential through the labored wit of intellectuals. Joyce makes this point when he shows Bloom to be for opposite reasons an outsider at both gatherings.

Paradox is also the hallmark of Stephen's conversation and thought, but not of his alone. In "Scylla and Charybdis," one of Wilde's gravest and most incriminating paradoxes (his theory that Shakespeare's sonnets were written for one Willie Hughes) is humorlessly defended by the Quaker Lyster: "Do you think it is only a paradox . . . The mocker is never taken seriously when he is most serious." (199) On which Stephen, paradoxically assuming Mulligan's role as mocking chronicler of Dublin's literati, reflects, "They talked seriously of mocker's seriousness." For Joyce, who left Ireland so that he could create his country out of himself, paradox is generally both real and apparent like the frequent incongruous-seeming juxtapositions and the idea of taking as his model for the all-city the down-at-the-heel capital of a subject province imbued with a sense of its glorious past and dormant potential. But real and apparent paradox have always been the stock-in-trade of religious thinkers, mystics, and poets, and, as Joyce repeatedly suggests, Jerusalem in Christ's time was an eastern Dublin, smarting under the heel of Rome.

Like just about every other aspect of *Ulysses,* paradox is both a method and theme, contributing to stasis and motion. Seen as negation, that is, as a cancelling out of one item by its contrary, it is equivalent to paralysis, another of Joyce's favorite themes and a term applied to the Dublin of *Dubliners.* The idea of the dropsical ruin of a "citizen" leading a revolution is a case in point, as is the view of Ireland hoping to win the status of a new power by turning back the clock. On the other hand we have the portrait of a Bloom, complete from dandruff to piles, as the norm for humanity, or we have Stephen sharing and systematically reversing the thoughts of his antitype. In these instances, despite apparent absurdities, neither term of the paradox is cancelled out, though both are altered to good effect, a dynamic balance is achieved. We can point also to the medial nature of Bloom's attributes and to the fact that, without identifying with him, we sense repeatedly that he is doing and feeling as we might. Hence the further paradox that we find ourselves attuned against our will to the nature of the undistinguished failure. This is the sort of reaction that a satirist might hope to inspire, but Joyce's book is only marginally satirical.

The parallelism of Stephen's thought with Bloom's is more than the product of novelistic license which permits coincidence, if not opposite equivalence, as a structural device. Their paired reflections do more than emphasize their complementary dispositions. They produce a fruitful tension and a Janus-faced awareness which will be stored in our communal mind in readiness for the indiscriminate thought-texture of "Circe." In "Aeolus," Bloom, ever objective in his response, but just recently returned from the funeral, watches the presses and reflects with gruesome logic on machines and men, conjoining with paradoxical effect organic and inorganic images:

> Machines. Smash a man to atoms if they got him caught. Rule the
> world today.[11] His machineries are pegging away too. Like these, got
> out of hand: fermenting. Working away, tearing away. And that old
> grey rat tearing to get in. (118)

There are echoes here from Stephen's ghastly projection in "Proteus" of the putrefying corpse of the drowned man, whose fate calls
to mind nature's economy. (50) But more powerful echoes occur in
"Wandering Rocks," where a cosmic catastrophe is generated in
Stephen's mind by the sight of Old Russell at his lapidary wheel
and the sound of "dynamos from the powerhouse":

> Beingless beings. Stop! Throb always without you and the throb
> always within. Your heart you sing of. I between them. Where?
> Between two roaring worlds where they swirl, I. Shatter them, one
> and both. But stun myself too in the blow. Shatter me you who
> can. (242)

Images, ideas, and impulses are parallel. Both men accommodate
the circumstance to their concerns and personalities, but Bloom has
rendered the machines as organisms while Stephen has turned from
machine and organism to the cosmos. Bloom is engaged by a world
that Stephen is determined to turn into a metaphor. Stephen's
"roaring worlds" are mental and personal, Bloom's interacting gears
are physical and impersonal. Both men are aware of the impulse to
dominate and both are repulsed by force, but Bloom masters his fear
by capitulating to it while Stephen increases his terror by pretending
to meet force with force. Even the sense of motion is opposite. Bloom
sees piston action and rasping, while Stephen sees and feels rotation
and collision. Two very different minds, moved by a similar stimulus
and expressing their concern in opposite ways, become ironically
identified in our minds while remaining distinct and unreconcilable.

Joyce's rigorous use of apparent paradox is a major source of
Ulysses' charm, as is its quality as a self-perpetuating puzzle, a port-
able infinity symbol. It is also a source of exasperation for readers
eager to conclude; for though it can readily vitalize even the most
trivial event, thought, or identity, it will not fix or define, and it
acts as a solvent for conclusions. Thus, in terms of his realistic
context, Joyce is playing an interesting double game. On the one
hand he does everything he can to render immediate the circumstances of his Dublin world, to engross us in the fates of his protagonists. We are almost as eager to see things turn out well on June 16
as we are to see the hero of melodrama succeed or fail. After all we
have invested much time and emotion in the protagonists' nature.

But Joyce obliges us to see them from a distance, even when we are engaged by their minds. He constantly opposes them to more attractive characters or exposes them in repulsive or unpleasant acts or juxtaposes them so that they expose each other or suggests absurdly appropriate analogies.

IV

Where does this leave us at the end of the day? Certainly, Stephen will not always be a young man or an irresolute one. On the other hand, he probably will not establish any sort of liaison with Molly or function as a replacement for Bloom's lost son. Still, we may question the impact of the two sorts of violence in "Circe," the inner and the outer, the degree of Stephen's liberation from the tendencies not of a day but of a lifetime, and the significance of the meeting with Bloom. Is the positive act of refusing Bloom's offer a sign that Stephen has been altered? It is certainly the first and only decision he comes to, though his motives are obscured by the chapter's technique. As for Bloom, the degradation he experiences with mixed bliss and horror in "Circe" will not work any permanent miracle, or even measurably increase his self-awareness, though it seems to have rendered possible and plausible his behavior in the rest of the book. His dream of a future association with Stephen is on a level with his travel plans and his literary ambitions. His cuckolding is confirmed and silently accepted. As a result of his request for breakfast in bed, Molly lets her thoughts drift back to a relationship she has taken for granted and contemplates a gross seduction patterned after the "Circe" visions before she mellows into her reaffirmation of their romance. All of this has a nice conclusive ring, but what does it mean?

Joyce's chapters, most particularly the nocturnal ones, are full of "turning points," lesser moments of decision and recognition, but then every instant is both a moment of change and a continuation of the unbroken process of identity, the actualization of the possible. This is what Stephen means when, drunken and out of sorts, he reacts to Lynch's mocking reference to Bruno[12] by paraphrasing Maeterlinck:[13]

What went forth to the ends of the world to traverse not itself. God, the sun, Shakespeare, a commercial traveller, having itself traversed in reality itself, becomes that self . . . Self which it itself was ineluctably preconditioned to become. (505)[14]

Though perhaps too solipsistic, this view suggests the sort of process underlined both by the paradoxes and analogies and the treatment of action in *Ulysses*. (It also motivates Stephen's despair by ruling out choice and obviating decision.) Under the circumstances it would require extraordinary ingenuity to define unequivocally Joyce's attitude toward an event or to establish anything as crucial. Yet the question will bear a closer look.

Two recent critics draw consolation from "Ithaca." Returning to his bed, Bloom finds in his place "the imprint of a human form, male, not his, some crumbs, some flakes of potted meat, recooked, which he removed." (731) The laconic catechist proceeds to expose Bloom's reactions beginning with his smile at the thought of the twenty-four oddly assorted males whom he imagines to have preceded Boylan and then analysing his "antagonistic sentiments": "Envy, jealousy, abnegation, equanimity." (732) For Arnold Goldman the sequence suggests that Bloom has graduated from the Kierkegaardian "ethical" phase to his "religious" phase, that is, that he has achieved a degree of spiritual elevation.[15] For Clive Hart, "Bloom has reached a state of equanimity about the act of adultery itself."[16] Both critics are concerned with a possible but intangible development, which can perhaps be measured in terms of "Sirens," where Bloom unheroically saddened reacts to the melodramatic stimulus of a patriotic song, "The Croppy Boy":

> I too, last my race. Milly young student.[17] Well, my fault perhaps.
> No son. Rudy. Too late now. Or if not? If not? If still? [18]
> He bore no hate.
> Hate. Love. Those are names.[19] Rudy. Soon I am old. (285)

Here, caught on the wing, is the "resignation" if not the "equanimity," in relation not only to the adultery but to all of his concerns. "Ithaca" shows us that Bloom has borne up under the fact of the expected discovery of Molly's infidelity pretty much as expected, though he has briefly considered other expedients. Hart's view is closer to reality than Goldman's, which hangs (ironically) upon a possible analogy, but Goldman's (if it is accepted as analogy) is more like the sort of change one would expect in so paradoxical a book. Both posit a slight if not equivocal conclusion to a day of striving. Neither is truly conclusive and both are weakened by the context, which includes as justification for Bloom's attitude the dubious list of suitors. If Bloom really believes in the frequency of Molly's affairs, we may assume that he has felt the "antagonistic sentiments" before. If he doesn't believe in it, what validity do the sentiments have?

So much for Bloom's personal development. What about his relationship to Stephen? Before they part the two men indulge "at Stephen's suggestion, at Bloom's instigation" (702) in a most private act which is echoed on the cosmic level by the trajectory of a falling star.[20] Without denying or affirming the significance of the moment, Joyce produces the handy paradox. Males commonly urinate more or less together and Stephen has consumed a great deal of liquid, but since he has previously been less than warm if not quite cold, we may read his "suggestion" as a mildly friendly overture, a sign of gratitude or as Hart suggests a "recognition of common humanity."[21] Joyce has deliberately and comically befogged the issue by first having the two men stand silently "each contemplating the other in both mirrors of the reciprocal flesh of theirhisnothis fellowfaces." (702) This is a moment of equivocal recognition, but it seems to dissolve the joined reflection in "Circe." Then there is the micturition itself, described with the usual comic precision, and accompanied by thoughts that have little to do with a meeting of minds. Rather they could suggest a severance, and emphasize a distance which in fact has never been bridged. Bloom is thinking self-consciously of the qualities of his organ while Stephen is reflecting on circumcision as a probable consequence of Bloom's Jewishness but characteristically (and comically) in terms of the religious significance of Christ's foreskin: ". . . the carnal bridal ring of the holy Roman catholic apostolic church, conserved in Calcata. . . ." (703) We may be pleased to note that Stephen is thinking of someone other than himself, but we should not push that point too far, for he is treating and has treated Bloom as a source of information, and besides Joyce has another paradox at hand. According to the clearest statement on the subject, Bloom is uncircumcised (373), but since the two men circumspectly shield their members, Stephen cannot know this. Union? Communion? Understanding? Equanimity? In the absence of answers it is best not to conclude or to conclude in a variety of ways on various levels of the experience while keeping the analogies in mind as patterns for unrealized possibilities.

Perhaps this is what Joyce is suggesting when he defines the *wake*ing world of the dreamer of *Finnegans Wake* (who may be identical with the reader) as a "collideorscape," a kaleidoscopic landscape full of collisions and escapes. If so we may approach the Joycean universe armed with a sort of permutation theory. Since the world of each individual is subject to a great many but not an infinitude of changes, patterns will in the natural course of events repeat themselves, but since the moment is conditioned by those that precede or follow it, history "repeats itself with a difference." Thus a crucified Christ rejects paradise, the prodigal son rejects the father he has sought, and, as Joyce puts it in one of his notes, Ulysses is unlucky, Penelope is unfaithful. Whether we extend the metaphor to include mankind or apply it to a single individual (as for example Stephen, with whose pattern we are familiar from the *Portrait*), universals may be said to underlie all particulars and the least little act reverberates in history if not in the stars. In this perspective there can be no end, no solution, no resolution—only illusory fixes in which the components, like the bits and pieces of colored glass or paper in a kaleidoscope, seem to compose themselves into meaningful patterns which of necessity vanish before we have grasped their integrity or deciphered their implications.

V

FORM AND SURFACE

I

No one denies that *Ulysses* is, for better or worse, a technical *tour de force* though some regret the lengths to which Joyce went in elaborating this quality. S. L. Goldberg goes further than most:

> In parts of "Cyclops" or "Nausicaa," "Eumaeus," or even "Ithaca," for example, the energy of the writing is largely destructive, and it is elaborated too willfully to sustain our interest once we have taken the comparatively simple point it is making.[1]

On the surface this position is valid. Certain chapters strain our patience, almost as much as the biblical "begats," and work against the realistic context elaborated earlier, but we may ask if, in the total context, these are in fact flaws and if any aspect of *Ulysses* can be thought of as making a "simple point." Essentially, this is an attack on the later chapters, where Joyce abandons much of the paraphernalia of realism, but it includes as well a criticism of Joyce's self-indulgence (an unmeasurable quantity) and an attack aimed at the artist moving toward *Finnegans Wake* rather than the one moving from the *Portrait*. Such criticism suggests that a further step is necessary, an examination less of the much scrutinized devices as isolated phenomena than of the role of style and technique within a coherent structure, a look which could in its turn help illuminate other aspects of the book.

The time has passed when we could stop our consideration of Joyce's strategy with a discussion of the "stream of consciousness" technique. This, though fascinating in its details and possibilities, was neither completely original with Joyce, nor uniform, nor even dominant in *Ulysses*. There is no real reason to doubt that, though he clearly perfected and enlarged the technique, Joyce derived it most directly from Edouard Dujardin's novelette *Les Lauriers sont coupés* (*We'll to the Woods no More*), a copy of which he bought in a station in 1903.[2] He used the technique as he did many others to do specific jobs, and principally, to bring into unusually sharp focus the alert conscious minds of individuals whose character he wished to define quickly, completely, and unmistakably before dissolving individuality and disclosing the basis of character in hidden impulses.

Neither can we stop with a consideration of the homeric justification for the specific techniques or, for that matter, with a tabulation of the rhetorical devices in "Aeolus," a list of the models for Joyce's pastiches in "Oxen of the Sun," or an account of his "musical techniques" in "Sirens." Treatments of such ingenious effects, though in themselves engrossing, are rather like the explanations of jokes. They give more pleasure to the speaker than to the listener. The *Odyssey* supplied more and less than an expendable scaffolding. Too many of Joyce's effects were dictated by the analogy for us to ignore the rationale for such rewarding effects as the windy rhetoric of "Aeolus," the impertinent use of the "fuga per canonem" in "Sirens," the "gigantism" of "Cyclops," or the chunks of irregularly shaped prose fashioned for "Wandering Rocks." Though on a second reading we may feel that Joyce labors some of his tricks, we would not care to ignore their role as part of a discrete and ironical backdrop. Still, given the freedom with which he interpreted his models and taking into consideration the density of *Ulysses*, these analogies do not suffice to justify his literary pyrotechnics, explain his choices, or illuminate the impact of the styles on the reader.

As an innovator, with a passion for pulling the technical stops, Joyce broke violently with tradition when he decided for whatever reason to evolve fresh styles for each of his chapters and thus systematically fragment his narrative. But his passion for freedom was easily, though not obviously, dominated by a rage for order. This is reflected, to mention only a few of his controls, in the internal consistency of his chapters, in the graduated difficulty of his techniques, in the parallelism and interrelationship not only of characters, images, and analogies but even of chapter content, styles, and structures, and, in the narrational strategy and the evolution of a nameless creative persona or "arranger." I use the term "arranger" to designate a figure who can be identified neither with the author nor with his narrators, but who exercises an increasing degree of overt control over his increasingly challenging materials.

The early chapters modulate from a fairly conventional narrative, with stream of consciousness intrusions, toward the intricacies of Stephen's almost disembodied thought in "Proteus." From this we break into the lucid objectivity of Bloom's thoughtstream in "Calypso." With Bloom, a latterday Brobdingnag, we enter the ordinary world through the door of the familiar rendered strange. From chapter to chapter, though not with predictable rigor, the dose of stylistic strangeness is increased, building toward and accumulating energy for the outrage of "Circe." After slogging through the viscosity of "Eumaeus" we enter a frigid "Ithaca," from which Molly's harsh but palpitating humanity is a welcome relief. "Penelope" completes a circle, being virtually unpunctuated and completely unmediated in imitation of liquid flow, the seemingly random musings of a satisfied woman between dreams on a hot summer night. To support this chronological development, Joyce systematically introduced ironic echoes and imposed through style and structure formal tensions which reflect back on the action, regulating its flux, broadening and illuminating its significance.

Just as the two protagonists' developments are analogous and interrelated, though antithetical and distinct, the chapters relating parallel phases of their developments are often structurally and even stylistically parallel. But this is not enough. A given chapter will invariably be related to several others by subject matter, complexity, imagery, and even by length. "Proteus," in which Stephen reflects unsystematically on his condition, taking his cues from a static landscape, must be related to "Scylla and Charybdis." There, reflecting systematically within an ambiance made random by the conflicting voices, he constructs or rather reconstructs a meditation on Shakespeare, whose predicament is rendered analogous to his own. In terms of Joyce's schema, "Proteus," a "Monologue (male)," is balanced by the "Monologue (female)" of "Penelope." Virtually a soliloquy, it is in direct opposition to "Nestor." Focussed inward, it contrasts to the outgoing exuberance of Bloom's observations in "Calypso." It is more immediately related, however, by its subject matter and setting, to "Nausikaa." There Gerty and Bloom, each erotically preoccupied with himself in relation to another, sit during the "shepherd's hour" (379) where Stephen walked during "Pan's hour, the faunal noon." (49) Both "Proteus" and "Nausikaa," through their styles, their action, and their locale, hark back to and modify the climactic strand-stroll in chapter 4 of the *Portrait,* to Stephen's vision of daedalian flight, his anti-erotic voyeuristic moment with his muse and his blissful ("chaste") slumber.* Such rela-

---

* Stephen, who has been reminded of that moment by Mulligan's take-off in "Telemachus," feels no elation on Sandymount strand. Bloom, on the other hand, dramatizes the onanistic implications of Stephen's lyrical bird-girl experience by spending himself over a girl who is both lame and common. For opposite reasons, neither Stephen in the *Portrait* nor Bloom in *Ulysses* speaks to his love object, and both doze off after the experience. The *Ulysses* chapters in

tionships subtly blend the realms of reality and fancy, but they do not exhaust the stylistic play. Gerty's effusion reflects upon and balances "Penelope" to which it is the virginal response. It is also, like Bloom's "literary" manner in "Eumaeus," a thoroughly artificial performance that conveys for all its evasiveness the quality of an experience. As for Bloom, it is altogether appropriate that he meditate in "Nausikaa" as Molly does in "Penelope" on his own fleshcase. After all, at about this time Boylan is consummating his affair with the goddess of Bloom's dreams!

We find a similar constellation of chapters in "Scylla and Charybdis," "Cyclops," "Oxen of the Sun," and "Circe," all of which have elaborate overtones from the *Portrait*. The first three suggest, by virtue of their formats, symposia. All but "Oxen" are given near theatrical immediacy through style, though in each case the impact is as different as the narrative voice. All are carefully divided into acts and interludes. The second and third are full of parody and burlesque effects. Of course the parodies and burlesques in "Cyclops" are intrusive and unequivocally irreverent, though they tend to relate to as well as contrast with the action. Those in "Oxen" are organic but carefully shaded toward gravity in stark contrast to the tone of the proceedings. In "Cyclops," the most obvious humor is in the reaction; in "Oxen of the Sun," in the action. Similarly, "Scylla and Charybdis" shows the logical basis for the illogical action of "Circe," where Stephen's visions are perversely realized. Such interrelationships are as much an aspect of the arranger's role

---

contrasting styles combine to set Stephen's earlier moment in a new light. More significantly, Bloom is momentarily invested with Stephen's boyish identity ("Goodbye, dear. Thanks. Made me feel so young." (382)), while the Stephen of "Proteus" is rendered momentarily distant, harshly cynical, self-mocking, self-involved, the apparent opposite in fact of his younger romantic self:

> She trusts me, her hand gentle, the longlashed eyes.
> Now where the blue hell am I bringing her beyond the veil? Into the ineluctable modality of the ineluctable visuality. She, she, she. What she? The virgin at Hodges Figgis' window on Monday looking in for one of the alphabet books you were going to write. Keen glance you gave her. Wrist through the braided jess of her sunshade. She lives in Leeson park, with a grief and kickshaws, a lady of letters. Talk that to someone else, Stevie: a pickmeup. Bet she wears those curse of God stays suspenders and yellow stockings, darned with lumpy wool. (48–49)

We may contrast these remarks to Bloom's cool and wry but sympathetic appraisal of limping Gerty's lunar friskiness, but then Stephen's mood is changeable. In the next paragraph we find him relapsing into lush sensuality, accepting what he desires but fears will be denied: "Touch me. Soft eyes. Soft soft soft hand. I am lonely here." (49)

as the fact that both Bloom and Stephen are keyless this day; that Martha Clifford lives in Dolphin's Barn where Bloom courted Molly; that the Orangeman, Deasy, echoes the anti-Semitic sentiments of the proper Hibernophile Haines, while Mulligan shares attitudes with the all-Irish citizen; that the babysitter Bloom sees on the strand turns up as a whore in nighttown.

Finally, there are the larger structural implications. The three chapters of the "Telemachia," for example, are reflected in the temporally coterminous opening chapters of the "Odyssey" section, and in the "Nostos" which relates in its turn antithetically to the last three chapters of the central section. The central section, and hence the whole book, revolves around the eighteen plus one narrative fragments of "Wandering Rocks," a chapter unlike all the others in that it features Dublin rather than Bloom and Stephen and exposes the secret thoughts of three minor characters. It is more significant, however, that "Wandering Rocks" marks the beginning of the decline from daylight and social control into the license of the night, from the universe of clearly defined objects and ideas to the psychic space symbolized by two men urinating under the watchful stars and the soft-lit window of bedwarm Molly. The styles of the later chapters subtly mimic this development, providing an integral backdrop for the action and a commentary on it. Here balance is important. The night must not outweigh the day and the phases of the temporal and emotional journeys must have their appropriate weights (physical as well as rhetorical). A shorter or a more complex "Nausikaa" or a briefer and livelier "Ithaca" might spoil the "set" of this coat of many colors.

When morning finally closes the night of *Finnegans Wake* and the dream identities seem to vanish, the narrator of the last chapter decrees that "every crisscouple [will] be so crosscomplimentary . . . in a farbiger pancosmos." But concerning the difference between the dream and waking worlds, he tells us, "Yet is no body present here which was not there before. Only is order othered. Nought is nulled." [3] The crisscrosscomplimentary people of *Ulysses* have less far to travel than does the dream-reader of *Finnegans Wake,* but allowance made for the difference in scale, the same applies to the night world as opposed to the day world of Stephen and Bloom: "only is order othered." Joyce's problem was to suggest and enforce the impression of the interrelatedness and the opposition of the night and day consciousness, the unity of mankind and the uniqueness of individuals. The problem was a delicate one. On the one hand, he had to convey the multi-personal reality within the orderly frame of daily life in a large city. On the other, he wished to bring together under one hat his antitypes without doing violence to the logic of experience. He had already evolved ways of disclosing the nature of the individual. Here he would go further, exhibiting as well qualities that underlie and undercut individuality, the common substratum of historical and psychic experience. It is through the direct representation of subconscious urges in relation to an implied historical reality[4] that the "father" and the "son" will be identified and joined while being confirmed in their singularity.

In the *Portrait,* Joyce had to convey the quality of a developing mind and an evolving identity, to justify its evolution in terms of experience, to draw, that is, a true portrait. Since, in line with the traditions of Flaubertian realism, he chose to write in an objective narrative voice (one through which the author's will is conveyed indirectly), he had to evolve styles which are mimic approximations of the mental rhythms of the growing boy, further justifications for his ultimate condition, and corollaries to the action. The problem was immensely more complex in *Ulysses* where space as well as time had to be dealt with and where he had to modulate from one sort of consciousness to another, from unity in diversity to diversity in unity. Like the distances travelled by Homer's heroes, the distances between day and night, outer and inner experience, Stephen and Bloom, the individual and the community, are incalculable. It was not a question of how to convey a natural process but rather how to combine without dilution contradictory modes. A physical and emotional impossibility had to be made plausible on a spiritual level. To accomplish this Joyce contrived to develop *in extenso* the characters' daytime contexts, stressing the clarity of Stephen's thought and Bloom's observations before immersing both in a worldly context which he renders increasingly unrealistic and distant so that he can take us through and beyond the shadow play on the inner stage of the mind. In the later chapters Joyce's means seem to take over and the reader finds himself more obviously engaged by the esthetic surface which must ultimately serve not as a barrier but as a means of access to the drama within. Increasingly, he accepts a position halfway between the artist and his creation. As a creator engaged in the mechanics of the novel, he is capable of apprehending the vitality of the underlying order; as a spectator engaged by the characters' predicaments, he participates in their nature, from which he has been so carefully distanced. To understand and appreciate this minor miracle we must investigate the manipulation of the narrative voice, the evolving chapter techniques, and the intricacies of style on the level of the passage.

II

Though we may be dazzled by the virtuosity of the artistic prime mover, we need not overlook a certain comforting consistency in the persona behind the action of the first eleven chapters. It is in small effects that his presence is first felt, in stylistic ticks or rather rhetorical gestures which add point, interest, and humor to what might otherwise be bland descriptive passages connecting bits of dialogue or monologue. Quite apart from its content, each of the following brief citations has some locution in it that speaks for the narrator's particular brand of exuberance:

He tore the flower gravely from its pinhold smelt its almost no smell. . . . (78)

The dead flower removed from Martha's letter during "Lotus Eaters" is endowed by the narrator with a comically poetic near-absence of smell. Again, the turn of phrase and the word choice set up a delightfully spurious tension. The overtone of violence in the act of tearing and in the "pinhold" are underscored by the adverb "gravely," which gives the action an absurdly funereal quality. We may compare the "almost no smell" to the "nocoloured eyes looking through the glasses" of the sadistic Father Dolan in the *Portrait*.[5]

Mr. Bloom nodded gravely, looking in the quick bloodshot eyes. (105)

In keeping with the funeral context of "Hades," the narrator contrasts Bloom's *grave* nod with Mr. Kernan's "quick bloodshot eyes." A characteristic device is the double and perhaps triple reference of "gravely," which qualifies both verb and participle and rebounds against "quick," which is in turn qualified by "bloodshot." These eyes are quick with the life of the moribund, since, like Dignam, who died of drink, Kernan is a "lush."

KYRIE ELEISON!

A smile of light brightened his darkrimmed eyes, lengthened his long lips.
—The Greek! he said again. *Kyrios!* Shining word! (133)

Here again are balanced opposites, in this case the components of Professor MacHugh's smile. The narrator's signature is on the "smile of light" which refers as much to the "shining" vowels of the Greek word as to the quality of MacHugh's expression. (Exceptionally, the headline seems to be both a summary of the action and a part of the dialogue.) The smile exposes no teeth and the light is confined to the eyes which are by contrast "darkrimmed." The language almost cancels out the joy, and the light rhyme effects with which the sentence opens are weighted by the heavy Anglo-Saxon alliteration with which it ends. Not surprisingly, the Greek is being compared to the Semite and Saxon. Though the sentence's rhetorical density is appropriate to Stephen's thought patterns and to the context ("Aeolus"), the narrator remains virtually identical with the speaker in the other passages.

> Mr. Best entered, tall, young, mild, light.
> He bore in his hand with grace a notebook, new, large, clean, bright. (186)

These two sentences from "Scylla and Charybdis" have the impact of a good pantomime sequence or a Beerbohm caricature. More obtrusive than the earlier examples, they inevitably, if pleasantly, distract us from the dense fabric of the argument they interrupt. The balanced strings of adjectives, the terminal rhymes, the unpretentious monosyllables suggest the effort of a turn of the century schoolboy poet as well as the manners of a modern Ganymede whose appearance gives Stephen his next irreverent point. Though different in spirit from the other examples, these absurdly scannable lines represent a mood of the narrator, the comic aside of one who is capable of expressions like "turned an unoffending face" or "repeated to John Eglinton's newgathered frown." (187)

> By the stern stone hand of Grattan, bidding halt, an Inchicore tram unloaded straggling Highland soldiers of a band. (228)

Meter, alliteration, half-rhyme, and synecdoche contribute to the rigid effect of Grattan's statue seen as a "stern stone hand" before the sentence crumbles into flat-footed prose to imitate the movement of the "straggling Highland soldiers" only to close with a lagging rhyme: "of a band."

> Bore this. Bored Bloom tambourined gently with I am just reflecting fingers on flat pad Pat brought. (279)

In "Sirens" the narrator loses ground. As in this sentence, his voice is refined into "musical" prose complete with puns, facile rhymes, alliteration, onomatopoeia. Though it is still recognizable as a vehicle capable of recording actual events and reactions, it is more audacious (see the "I am just reflecting fingers"), weaving together bits of overheard lyrics, thought fragments, and snatches of conversation to convey a total musical context. There is no fixed point of view.

After "Sirens" the narrator practically disappears, leaving behind a babble of voices but returning flittingly in Bloom's section of "Nausikaa" (379), or intruding occasionally in "Eumaeus," and more often in "Ithaca." In "Circe" Joyce reverses the naturalistic procedures by accurately describing illusions, or, as in the following passage, magically transforming tawdry nature:

> Rows of flimsy houses with gaping doors. Rare lamps with faint rainbow fans. Round Rabaiotti's halted ice gondola stunted men and women squabble. They grab wafers between which are wedged lumps of coal and copper snow. Sucking, they scatter slowly. Children. (429)

This description of houses with glowing fanlights and open doors on a dim-lit street is rendered more eerie by a speaker whose directions are meant to disorient us, who colors his details with words like "gaping," "faint," "stunted," "squabble" before he naturalizes the scene with a word: "Children." We have come a long way from the technique evident in the description of "two carfuls of tourists [which] passed slowly, their women sitting fore gripping frankly the handrests. Pale faces. Men's arms frankly round their stunted forms." (228) The "stunted forms" so succinctly presented by the narrator of "Wandering Rocks," whose point of view is momentarily Stephen's, are frankly incongruous, objects of open ridicule. In "Circe" the magical playwright speaks to us from our own point of view, and the creatures whom we are fooled into seeing as grotesques discomfort us as part of an unnatural landscape into which we are drawn by a web of illusion.

The narrator of the early chapters with his marked concern for the word and its mutative powers and his relatively objective stance operates as a brake on the very flux his language generates if only because his voice is consistent. He also contributes a randomness of his own which foreshadows the intricate perspectival ambiguities of "Circe." A striking example of this is the following passage from "Telemachus," a telegraphic description of Mulligan dressing before Stephen, who reflects on what he sees:

> He emptied his pockets on to the table.
> —There's your snotrag, he said.
> And putting on his stiff collar and rebellious tie, he spoke to them, chiding them, and to his dangling watchchain. His hands plunged and rummaged in his trunk while he called for a clean handkerchief. Agenbite of inwit. God, we'll simply have to dress the character. I want puce gloves and green boots. Contradiction. Do I contradict myself? Very well then, I contradict myself. Mercurial Malachi. A limp black missile flew out of his talking hands.
> —And there's your Latin quarter hat, he said. (16–17)

There is no way of knowing what is said as opposed to what Stephen thinks of this dumb show sandwiched between the two presentations. Whether or not Buck speaks while his hands gesture is moot. The second half of the paragraph is a curious amalgam of possible and improbable utterance, some of which (like "Agenbite of inwit") is surely Stephen's, some of which may be remembered utterance, and again some, like the quotation from Whitman ("Do I contradict . . . myself"), may be a favorite tag. We have entered a dead space between thought and action, and, no matter how vivid the pantomime, we have a sense that the two individuals are momentarily and magically joined by the narrator whose procedures are more comprehensible on the thematic and analogical levels than on the mimetic. In this way he has foreshadowed the more emphatic miracle by which Bloom and Stephen are joined in Circe's looking-glass. By making a character address objects, letting hands talk, a hat fly, a tie rebel, creating, that is, out of the absurdities latent in our diction an enchanted landscape which we accept without question, he has also foreshadowed a more radical dislocation of reality. The muzziness in our citation is then deliberate. The narrator is obliging us to accept another order of reality. He is playing on our need to naturalize and explain the strange and elusive, to close the field of experience. He is also asserting his independence, his freedom from the rules he himself has established. Gradually and with calculated stealth this invisible but consistently identifiable speaker will be metamorphosed into the artist-God as cosmic joker, the other side of Stephen's "hangman god." By the book's second half he will have become a creature of many faces but a single impulse, a larger version of his characters with a larger field of vision and many more perceptions to control, the figure I am calling the arranger.

The structural rhythm of the book, echoing and miming the "dance of the hours," is one of Joyce's most startling achievements and the greatest single justification for his style shifts. But the nature of this rhythm and the qualities that make it possible for Joyce to give coherence to a frame that can accommodate literary and psychic extremes can be understood only through a systematic study of Joyce's techniques for each chapter.

III

The first six chapters of *Ulysses* must be considered as a unit. They prepare the reader through dramatic exposition for the thematic concerns of the entire novel, through modifications in the techniques

for the more radical style shifts of the later chapters, through the increasing use of the stream of consciousness for the phasing out of the
conscious personal voice in the evening chapters. Stephen's point of
view complemented by that of a sympathetic narrator dominates the
first three chapters, Bloom's the next three. These chapters contain
the clearest exposition and correspond to the four most clear-headed
hours of the day. "Telemachus" and "Hades" are social or group
chapters which might be qualified as dramatic units. In contrast to
the narrowly focussed *Portrait*, which it nevertheless continues,
"Telemachus" presents each of the characters in a witty but objective
light from a vantage point that is not necessarily Stephen's. Stephen's
voice, which was first heard in the diary entries that conclude the
Portrait, is here rendered as a secondary but more immediate commentary on action to which it is set in opposition and from which he
feels excluded. His comments, concluding with the bitter "Usurper,"
are a source of unresolved tension. A secondary tension derives from
the narrator's suggestive presentation through which a multitude of
images and allusions manifest themselves. "Nestor" and "Lotus
Eaters" present Stephen and Bloom in the center of a larger dramatic frame and give their voices and reactions clear precedence.
In "Nestor" the narrator fades to present everything through
Stephen's eyes, acting more emphatically as a complement to his
reactions. As a result, the other characters become as they have been
in the *Portrait*, extensions of Stephen's experience. Stephen stands
suspended between young "ignorance" and old "wisdom" as a middle
term. His stream of consciousness, in keeping with the educational
setting, is so highly organized and rich in historical allusions that he
seems to control the machinery of suggestion. "Proteus" and
"Calypso" are the protagonists' most isolated performances. In
"Proteus" the narrator's voice complements Stephen's self-conscious
musings, making possible such effects as the Paris flashback or the
visit to Uncle Richie. Stephen's voice, which at times blends inextricably with the narrator's, has become a protean instrument capable of a wide range of moods and effects, accurately reflecting his
inner confusion but in a self-conscious and bookish style.

Like "Proteus," "Calypso" presents the character's (Bloom's) ambiance in terms of his reactions. But here the narrator is a counter-
persona. While Bloom reacts sardonically or humorously to aspects
of his environment, the narrator is gently ironic about Bloom and
through his treatment of details puts the Bloomish mentality into
sharper relief. Bloom himself presents details with objective clarity
in contrast to the subjective clarity of "Proteus." We are bombarded
not with crystalline thought but with objects and actions each of

which stands out against the field into which it will quickly blend. His thoughtstream, at once flexible and more natural, seems to have less inner coherence: a jumble of vivid and intimate details is thrown at us before we are properly introduced to our man.

"Lotus Eaters" puts Bloom in a more populous setting, permits him to react to more varied stimuli. Here, as in "Nestor," the narrator withdraws, becoming almost invisible, but returning occasionally to comment on details. In this, one of the more effective homeric chapters, the theme of torpid euphoria is echoed by the relaxed tone which mutes the eventful texture of the prose. Whereas in "Calypso" the narrator provided a comic counterpoint for Bloom's gentle humor, here Bloom is allowed to expose his own foibles while commenting on those of others. Two meetings (with M'Coy and Bantam Lyons) break the narrative, introducing voices that contrast with Bloom's, giving him a chance to comment within a more dynamic context.

The real contrast comes with "Hades" where Bloom's voice, though still dominant, is supplemented by dialogue. Here his humor becomes distinctly morbid and his voice increasingly subjective. The public and the private rhythms are boldly juxtaposed and the narrator once more stands above the scene registering the action and moving out into the world so that other characters can comment on Bloom. Thus for the first time he introduces a secondary dramatic dimension. Bloom is a part of this scene in much the same way Stephen is a part of the action of "Telemachus," [6] with this significant difference: Stephen is a grave and severely distanced protagonist, while Bloom is a comic character to whom we have begun to be attached.

In "Aeolus," the first chapter which Stephen and Bloom share, Joyce begins to undermine his narrative voice. The whimsical headlines assert a counter-nature to the objective persona, reminding us of the deliberate clowning of Sterne's Tristram Shandy, that early example of the self-shaping literary mind. Intrusive but not disruptive, these sardonic interjections break the rhythm of the chapter only to the degree that they usurp space within a temporally continuous context. Though most of the chapter is given over to dialogue, the narrator's voice is marked and consistent whether the passage relates to Bloom or Stephen. The stream of consciousness, on the other hand, after a by now typical opening, is muted in the second half of the chapter, where Stephen takes part in the conversation. For technical as well as strategic reasons no attempt is made to juxtapose Stephen's and Bloom's thoughtstreams here or anywhere else in the novel. Interestingly, at the crucial second encounter with

Crawford, Bloom's thoughts suddenly return to the page, registering his reaction not only to the rebuff but also to Stephen. (145) On the other hand, at an equally crucial moment for Stephen, the spinning of the bitterly ironic "Parable of the Plums," we have no record of his thought, or rather only the most sketchy and inconclusive record.

It is with some surprise and perhaps a bit of relief that we return in "Lestrygonians" to Bloom's stream of consciousness and the discreet and more than usually objective narrator. This use of an established convention is part of the alternate motion of the book's styles which invariably become more conservative before Joyce pushes on to new experiments. Effectively, "Lestrygonians" provides a buffer between "Aeolus" and "Scylla," which shocks us the more after the pause. (A similar tactic is noticeable in "Nausikaa," a placid contemplative interlude between two outrageous and hectic chapters.) The proliferating food and eating allusions that buttress the homeric analogy are not intrusive. Once again the monologue is broken by encounters, and, as in "Hades," the narrator wanders off to gather comments on Bloom, this time from disinterested and favorable parties.

"Aeolus" has prepared us for the more emphatic but subtler manipulations in "Scylla and Charybdis," where Joyce pits Stephen's increasingly lighthearted argument against his growing inner despair. In terms of the action this contrast is pointed up when the sober and mystical AE exits shortly before an insouciant and ribald Mulligan enters to set a new tone. (Mulligan's farcical intrusion recalls Alcibiades' riotous entrance after Socrates' discourse in the *Symposium,* a parallel reinforced in Joyce's schema by a reference to Socrates and by the "technic" of this chapter: "dialectics.") The chapter is written in a medley of styles appropriate to the variety of functions it serves. At its center is the argument itself, rendered in the precise words of the participants, each of whom is characterized by a particular intellectual position and therefore by a particular rhetoric. Beyond this there is Stephen's playful but tense stream of consciousness loaded with freight for the argument, larded with ironic perceptions, increasingly private, but throughout, a fascinating performance. The narrator's relatively objective voice is complemented by a sharper, irreverent commentator reflecting on the action from Stephen's point of view. This puckish commentator contributes, not only the caricatural asides, but also the increasingly numerous typographical eccentricities: the dramatic dialogue that conveys Stephen's playful mood (203),[7] the second sequence in dialogue (209), which contains nothing to justify its format, and Mulligan's *dramatis personae* (216–17), which is in contrast with and completes Best's playbill (187). Such devices suggest that the subject matter of the discussion is in itself dramatic and underscore the dramatic quality of Stephen's commitment to an argument he knows to be fruitless.

Up to "Wandering Rocks" the stream of consciousness has given us an approximation of two minds unraveling themselves in relation to a world full of opacities. Now the arranger begins to reduce these protagonists to the condition of the other characters, obliging us to reorient ourselves so that we may use our knowledge of Stephen and Bloom in contexts where their thought is jumbled, distorted, or absent. For the first and last time some of the minor characters come to us through their streams of consciousness (in Conmee's case mixed with indirect discourse). The strategy enables Joyce to present ironic foils for Stephen in little Dignam, who is also in mourning, for Bloom in the ineffectual commercial traveler Mr. Kernan, and for both together in Conmee, a figure who connects the two protagonists, being both a fatherly older man and religious in his orientation. This pivotal chapter is informed by cinematic montage which conveys a sense of simultaneity within a clearly delineated geographical space through a series of interlocking prose vignettes. The controlling image is the viceregal cavalcade (the State); the narrative thread is Father Conmee's progress across town (the Church). Both are seen in relation to the city and its concerns.[8] Throughout this chapter we are aware of being manipulated by the arranger, who insists on the spatial dimension by inserting incongruous reminders and breaking continuity to suggest the spontaneous rhythm of life seen in passing. Still, in sequence after sequence the narrator's voice gives us slight genre paintings, fragmentary in effect but complete in the manner of the epiphanies, and firmly anchored in other aspects of the book. The chapter ends with a playful list of variously engaged spectators, enlivened by delightful and inappropriate details.

Beginning with the contrasting metallic notes of "Bronze by gold" and ending like the chapter with the patriotic "eppripfftaph" of Bloom's innocent anal salute, the overture of "Sirens" is a treasury of phrases torn from the chapter in order of their appearance. A fitting complement to the playful list of spectators at the viceregal procession, it also sets the tone of this chaotic-seeming chapter by giving musical or at least onomatopoetic form and rhythmic diversity to prosaic circumstance. "Sirens" also prolongs the technique of "Wandering Rocks" by weaving the movements of Bloom, Boylan, and the blind stripling into the texture of the bar scene. It goes far beyond "Scylla" in integrating (or orchestrating) events occurring in different parts of the bar, interrelating through verbal *legerdemain* unrelated actions. This is possible because, as in the following passage, the arranger irreverently but consistently distorts the rhythm of the narrative voice:

> Bloowho went by by Moulang's pipes, bearing in his breast the sweets of sin, by Wine's antiques in memory bearing sweet sinful words, by Carroll's dusky battered plate, for Raoul.
> The boots to them, them in the bar, them barmaids came. For them unheeding him he banged on the counter his tray of chattering china. And (258)

Here the two dimensions (Bloom "bearing . . . the sweets of sin" and the boots bearing a tray of tea), despite the misleading reference and the dislocations, are explicit enough but the events themselves are subjected to reduction and condensation. As a result of this technique, the reader is fully engaged by the verbal surface as an independent source of events and interest. While forcing us to work harder and depriving us both of a firm narrative perspective and of Bloom's dependable voice, Joyce is working more than ever against himself. His dislocations are possible and effective, however, because we have accumulated an awareness of Bloom's mind and the Dublin scene. It is fitting that when Bloom's concerns come back into focus even his thoughts are rendered comically random, captured, so to speak, by the sirens' music to which he responds by picking up themes or falling into a mental lilt.

Perhaps the most startling thing Joyce could do after the verbal extravagance of "Sirens" was to reverse himself, returning not only to the narrative tradition but apparently to oral narrative on a very low popular level. "Cyclops" is sheer outrage and fun in all of its details, from the unidentified narrator, a cyclopean drink-cadging dun out of the middle depths of Dublin, to the balloon-popping interludes burlesquing a variety of subliterary genres. These asides are not part of the action, yet they grow naturally out of the context on which they comment so directly and expansively. Though they break the narrative rhythm, they do not distort the circumstance which reduces Bloom to an opacity if not a cliché, the scorned outsider whose increasing discomfort in the face of innuendo can only be surmised since we do not hear his thoughts. His behavior comes to us glossed by a character who knows how to spice a tale with malice:

> And Bloom, of course, with his knockmedown cigar putting on swank with his lardy face. Phenomenon! The fat heap he married is a nice old phenomenon with a back on her like a ballalley. (305)

This is the voice of Dublin giving us, for all its hyperbolic language, the "straight dope," a voice appropriate to low comedy, a genial mocker. It is also the voice of HCE's opponent in *Finnegans Wake*, Hosty, the down-and-outer who composes a scurrilous song to expose him to public scorn. The pace of the action itself is slow, the development rational, but the chapter reads, thanks to the comic trappings, like a farcical expansion of the muddled thought of the citizen and his drunken cronies. It contains Joyce's bitterest and broadest satire.

After the double-decked mockery of "Cyclops," the gentle mock-pastoral of "Nausikaa" seems tame, a rest for Bloom and the reader. It contains only one major innovation, an artificial voice in indirect inner discourse. Accustomed to receiving the unmediated thought-stream, we are surprised and amused by this further breach of faith, but we have entered a stereotyped world and the sugary rhetoric is in keeping with the preciosity of the matter. Like the nude nymph on the Blooms' bedroom wall, Gerty is a figment of the male imagination even in her own eyes: a product, that is, of her wish to charm and of the religious training that has left her emotionally deprived. To emphasize this, Joyce interlards her monologue with snatches from the mass and permits Bloom to react in his own somewhat sweetened voice only after she has left. In order to join stylistically the opposite visions of Bloom and Gerty, Joyce narrates the whole chapter in a fittingly overripe prose. The "technic" is "tumescence detumescence," but with characteristic irony the swelling male role is given to a virgin and Bloom is left with the post-masturbatory mess. The deflated prose follows the curve of his fatigue.

"Nausikaa" mimes the perversion of sensibility. "Oxen of the Sun" deals, through its elaborate spoof on the history of English prose styles,* with the perversion of the intellect and the denial of nature. The tension between the rigidly stylized prose pastiches and the

---

* The limits of a particular style are worth noting and we may be engaged by Joyce's working out the problem of adjusting his styles to fit or contrast with the event and by the verve of his imitation. It should be noted that, just as there are arranger-intrusions in the narrator-controlled daylight chapters and *vice versa*, there are snatches of the later styles in the early passages. Stuart Gilbert explains this in terms of the irregular development of the embryo. The following rough list should help the reader find his bearings:[9]

Medieval Latin (383), Anglo-Saxon (384), Mandeville (386), Malory (387), Authorized Version and Browne (392), Bunyan (394), Pepys-Evelyn (396), Defoe (398), Swift (399), Addison (401), Sterne (404), Goldsmith (406), Burke (407), Junius (409), Gibbon (410), Radcliffe (412), Lamb (412), de Quincey (414), Landor (414), Macauley (416), Huxley (418), Dickens (420), Newman (421), Pater (422), Carlyle (423).

loose impiety and irreverence of the youths brings the reader further into the frame as an accomplice of the arranger, whose artificial disruption of the surface calls attention to his ingenuity. More important, the verbal texture, which impedes rather than facilitates our attempts to follow the action it adorns, hacks away at the very possibility of communication while conveying the simple circumstance through a variety of absurdly dated and variously appropriate literary postures. This strategy brings writers from the past back to life to comment on a present which casts their utterance in a fresh and generally comic light. However, the relationship of style to subject matter is not uniform. We may well question, for example, what is being deflated during the Dickensian and Carlylean commentaries on the Purefoys or how seriously we are to take Malory's Bloomish knight and Bunyan's characterization of Stephen as Boasthard. On the other hand, if many of the styles are inappropriately grave, some passages, especially those from the eighteenth century like the unforgettable Swiftian tale of the bull, are completely in keeping with the spirit of the moment. In a more general sense, designed to suggest the stages in the development of the embryo, the "technic" provides a useful bridge between the two timeless circumstances: the fecund but sterile wit of the roistering bucks and the pathetic parturition that brings yet another Purefoy into Catholic Ireland. Everything conspires to distract us from the characters' dilemmas, effectively limiting their viability as individuals. Though both Bloom and Stephen are present and Stephen contributes actively to the conversation before his place is usurped by the better clown Mulligan, it is only to Bloom's thoughts that we are attuned and these come to us mostly through a curtain of nineteenth-century styles. In "Circe," inner ferment will be conveyed as uproarious action; here, the din in the room is spoken about but not conveyed. Rather, the young men's exuberance and malice is stored up like the repressed concerns of Stephen and Bloom or like the tardy infant until, in the concluding passage, we burst the sack and the prose breaks out of its formal limits to become the direct if fragmentary expression of animal spirits. It is in these last pages, punctuated by the apocalyptic jargon of the American, Dowie, that most of the action occurs. But, if the earlier styles are often opaque, this literally transcribed but fragmentary utterance deprived of all narrational controls pulls us up short. What has occurred, if not precisely a riot, is an intellectual chaos appropriate to the drunken high spirits which bear psychic fruit in the next chapter.

"Circe," which places Bloom and Stephen as reactors to subconscious impulses in the center of an imaginary stage, combines techniques and effects from its literary models (*Faust* and *The Temptation of Saint Anthony*) with others from the traditional pantomime. Bloom and Stephen, after having been flattened out in the previous chapters are here emotionally inverted. The stage directions enable Joyce to project the contents of their minds on a screen of opaque and pedestrian activity. Even more striking is our sense that we are part of this scene, as baffled by the nightlight as they are, as bewitched. The nighttown context, for all of this, is kept clear enough so that we can divine, if we keep our eyes open, approximately where illusion meets fact. On the other hand, though the major hallucinatory sequences are carefully set off from each other and the chapter is artfully subdivided into dramatic acts and scenes, the arranger makes no clear distinction between minor hallucinations and the normal surface and even introduces improbable elements into the characters' hallucinations. As a result the visions and identities of Stephen and Bloom are blurred, universalized, mythicized; the components of their days are intermingled, so that their fates may momentarily be joined. Since the technique makes no formal distinction between the levels of experience, this was easy enough to accomplish. But the amount of fact, theme, and analogy juggling it required was staggering. Joyce seems to have taken the whole book, jumbled it together in a giant mixer and then rearranged its elements in a monster pantomime which, as is proper, includes every imaginable form of foolery but which may well be the most serious chapter in the book, a true rite of passage.

In "Eumaeus" we relapse from chaos to platitude in a tired, threadbare, flatulent narrative larded with the sort of commonplaces that would fill the mouth of Sancho Panza and please Flaubert. At University College Joyce delighted in the chronicle of Bouvard and Pécuchet, those two bumbling penpushers for whom Flaubert wrote his *Dictionary of Commonplaces*.[10] Here Joyce seems to be cramming all that the French writer knew on the subject into one short chapter which uses style to conceal sensibility but tickle the sense of humor. Like Flaubert, he ironically vindicates the norm (as opposed to the establishment) by demonstrating its capacity to generate a pathos that is beyond its comprehension. It is the voice and not the point of view that is Bloom's, and it is through the voice that the arranger conveys with surprising accuracy the drink- and fatigue-dulled sentiments of both protagonists. There is no stream of consciousness and only a hint of the early narrator, and despite the occasional nod toward Stephen, the chapter is dominated by Bloom's reflections on just about everything. The technique is parody only in the loosest sense, parody of a Bloomish mind turned inside out in a way that contrasts with the "Circe" inversion. It is a mind with its defenses up and not down, one which has turned suddenly public in the manner of a conventional and self-deceiving narrator. The result is ridiculous in a way that the stream of consciousness never is, but the point is not only that Bloom, like his style, is tired, but that the tired voice tries to convince us it has something to say.

In "Ithaca," the arranger, who has teased us through "Eumaeus," dons the mask of perverse objectivity. Like the "narrative (old)," the "catechism (impersonal)" seems precisely wrong for conveying a human situation and rewarding the reader who has warmed to the characters' predicament. Yet, in both chapters, the style permits Joyce to convey the inevitable resolution of an impossible relationship without resorting to brutal irony or maudlin sentiment. The questions and responses range from the most objective to the most personal, the language from the least to the most expressive. Increasingly, graphic passages function as seriocomic intrusions on the grave proceedings. In a sense this chapter, which, as though in an afterthought, carries so much of the book's exposition, is the warmest of them all. This is largely because despite his elaborate pose, the speaker is not completely reliable and his point of view is not always clear. He is after all a projection of Bloom's scientific mentality rather than of the spirit of inquiry pure and simple. For the first and only time we see Bloom and Stephen in conjunction as reactors, and we can measure the humanity of each on a minimal level which puts similarities and differences in sharp, humorous, and human relief. The technique is especially efficient at boiling down thought to the level of reflex, and in this sense both protagonists are comically stripped of their intellectual masks and rendered both vulnerable and human on a level at which Molly, however slight her motherly instinct, can approach and identify them.

After apparently draining his personae of all life, rendering them equal to the stars as constellated facts, distant and flickering, Joyce suddenly returns us to the earth in "Penelope." To accomplish this he concocted a medium designed to carry everything like the river Liffey in *Finnegans Wake,* which carries civilized humanity out to the sea for replenishment. Molly's monologue is an extreme form of stream of consciousness, so extreme that it brings us close to the conventions of the dramatic soliloquy in which the character must locate himself and describe his own behavior. Molly reacts to nothing but herself reacting to the recollected experience on a sensual level. Deprived of external controls, her monologue is apparently formless. Details and motives tend to flow together and personages to blend in ways that they cannot flow or blend anywhere else. Yet we can trace the development of Molly's thought, and we will automatically supply the missing punctuation so that Joyce has it both ways. Further, there are eight sentences which can be regarded as units of action. The openness of the form is comparable to the openness of "Circe" where themes and natures meet, identities are dissolved and blended. Here, on the other hand, character, the naturalistic sheath, is fixed, resolved, and related. The flowing prose of Molly reconstitutes, on a level that is less abstract than it has yet been, a reality mauled by the evening chapters. In the middle of the night we see many things clearly for the first time, as though from the other side of experience, by the light of the moon.

IV

The larger stylistic and technical shifts which mark the chapters of *Ulysses* are bound to attract more attention as symptoms of Joyce's virtuosity, and to demand more justification as functional aspects of the book. But a study of style and technique must not neglect the smaller units, the sentences, paragraphs and passages on which Joyce lavished such attention and which carry the main weight of his innovations and conceal, or rather reveal through suggestion, so many of the book's delights, far more in fact than any critic can disclose. An examination of almost any of these lesser segments is rather like a visit to the famous mausoleum of Galla Placidia in Ravenna, one of the gems of Italian Byzantine art. Entering a round chamber lit only by slits of windows paned with thin sheets of alabaster, we gaze about us at the vague mosaics that completely cover the inner walls and dome. Gradually, as our eyes accustom themselves to the light, details begin to appear, first the grosser and then the subtler, asserting themselves until they fill our sight beyond our capacity to apprehend them with a procession of sparkling images. If we allow for the difference in medium and the greater complexity of Joyce's vision, *Ulysses* is like a series of such chambers through which we pass rapidly, carrying with us images of all sorts in vital interaction and subject individually to further elaboration, images which, even half-seen, help compose our vision and create an impression of an organic whole. Though a comprehensive unraveling of the book would be impossible and probably counterproductive, it is well to look closely once in a while if only to appreciate the effects we have been subjected to and to apply our understanding to an appreciation of the book's subject matter. In this we return, as we must, to a unitary view of manner and matter and a sense of Joyce's total accomplishment.

We find some of Joyce's densest passages in the earlier, more conventional chapters. The following passage from "Telemachus" is remarkable for its alliterative effects, the deliberately repeated words and phrases (a common device in the *Portrait*), the curious perspectives and ambiguities designed to enforce juxtapositions, the shifts in mood and tone, and the synesthesia in May Dedalus' "mute, reproachful" "breath":

> —But a lovely mummer, he murmured to himself. Kinch, the loveliest mummer of them all.
> He shaved evenly and with care, in silence, seriously.
> Stephen, an elbow rested on the jagged granite, leaned his palm against his brow and gazed at the fraying edge of his shiny black coat-sleeve. Pain, that was not yet the pain of love, fretted his heart. Silently, in a dream she had come to him after her death, her wasted body within its loose brown graveclothes giving off an odour of wax and rosewood, her breath, that had bent upon him, mute, reproachful, a faint odour of wetted ashes. Across the threadbare cuffedge he saw the sea hailed as a great sweet mother by the wellfed voice beside him. The ring of bay and skyline held a dull green mass of liquid. A bowl of white china had stood beside her deathbed holding the green sluggish bile which she had torn up from her rotting liver by fits of loud groaning vomiting. (5)

This passage, simple enough for Joyce, is not free of elliptical phrases or ambiguous reference. What is the source of the "pain, that was not yet the pain of love"? Is it a sense of physical bereavement, or is it a reflection on friendship and betrayal, or again is it Stephen's own sense of the void of affection, his inability to achieve the distance from himself that would enable him to love another? Within a neat tripartite paragraph, we find a poignant opposition between the sunny scene and the morbid memory, between Stephen's self-concern reflected in the "threadbare cuffedge" and Mulligan's "wellfed voice." Playing against our expectations, Joyce gives us the "cuffedge" rather than the bay as the object of Stephen's gaze.

Skirting the thin edge of bathos or rather pushing beyond bathos, he counters the dream image ("in a dream she had come") with the gross details of the death throes, all the more moving because they are sparked by Mulligan's facile Swinburnean image of the sea as a "great sweet mother." (5) The carefully elaborated equation of the sea first to a bowl of vomit and then to death gives us in slow motion a foretaste of Stephen's stream of consciousness. The process is also mythologizing, for, by virtue of the highly charged language, the juxtaposition sea-mother-death-guilt-revulsion becomes at once unstable and indissoluble. From another point of view, the reader participates in a secondary creative process, being privy to the banal stimuli and the elaboration of an exceptional reaction which is not too far below the level of esthetic production. Joyce is forever emphasizing Stephen's role as the latent artist. At this point, however, as opposed to "Proteus," he is careful to give the words to the narrator, who weaves Stephen's impressions and characterizes for us a mind we have yet to inspect.

This is the first statement of the ghost-dream motive which partly motivates Stephen's distress and justifies his search for a mother substitute in the style of Ann Hathaway. The dream resolves itself finally in its hallucinated antistatement of "Circe" and finds its comic-pathetic counterpart in Bloom's vision of Rudy. But in this book of waking visions, the ghost-dream does not stand alone. Haines has dreamt of the "black panther," an identity later bestowed on Bloom. Bloom has dreamt of Molly in Eastern garb, a dream fulfilled imaginatively in "Circe" and realistically when Molly plans to buy herself such an outfit in "Penelope." Stephen has dreamt of meeting a man who offers him a melon and promises unknown pleasures, and this dream is fulfilled by his meeting with Bloom who offers him a liaison with Molly and who comically completes the action by his final "melonsmellonous osculation." (735) Stephen's dreams are respectively western (or of death and the night in relation to the sun's motion) and eastern (or of life and promise as reflected in Bloom's musings on the eastward journey in "Calypso").[11] (60–61)

By page six of *Ulysses,* the narrator who has spoken for Stephen and engaged us in his experience, begins to recede, allowing Stephen to speak for himself. In the following passage their voices almost imperceptively mingle:

> Stephen bent forward and peered at the mirror held out to him, cleft by a crooked crack, hair on end. As he and others see me. Who chose this face for me? This dogsbody to rid of vermin. It asks me too. (6)

Even before Stephen begins to speak to himself, the associative line has been established. He looks *at* the mirror before he looks in. He sees the crack with which he instinctively associates his own appearance and by extension his condition so that the two images blend and clash confusedly as would a single image viewed in a cracked glass. In accord with the image, the shift from objective to subjective utterance is abrupt but not jarring. Here too Stephen seems to be objective only about his own reflection. Later, we can contrast this "objectivity" with that of Bloom seeing himself through the eyes of his cat or in a variety of reflecting surfaces. Like the key, whose abandonment is one of the major symbolic actions of this chapter, and like the dreams, the mirror becomes a multivalent motif.

The question of identity and the related problem of parenthood are introduced when Stephen asks, "Who chose this face for me?" For Stephen, the face reflected in a mirror is but a shadow that can mask an identity, just as the body can provide the soul with a temporary case. Accordingly, physical relationships are unstable and Stephen's father, "man with my voice and my eyes" (38), and his sister Dilly ("My eyes they say she has . . . Shadow of my mind." (243)) should have no claims on him. As his reactions repeatedly show, however, he is unable to sever himself, to reject, in the manner of that fiery Irish saint Columbanus, or of Christ, the enforced relationship without severe conscience qualms, or "agenbite of inwit." His mask of strength is a mask for weakness. He holds too hard to the here and now to risk the necessary loss of an identity which is as yet insufficiently established. Thus we are brought back to the image in the split mirror, in which confused life is captured. Stephen's problem is then not one of simple acceptance or rejection but of how to accept and reject simultaneously, how to be of and above the world, how to be a creator, that is, one who projects out of his substance a new life which he does not live, an action which implies the acceptance of that substance in the first place. Thus he must face not only the reflection in the mirror but the image reflected, Stephen's "hair on end," his face, his "dogsbody to rid of vermin." The latter, a corollary to the vision of putrefaction in the dream passage examined earlier, underlines the nature of filth and vermin or of mortal misery, which he strives at great expense to surmount by the spirit. It is appropriate that in "Circe," in the midst of vital corruption Stephen first comes to grips with his identity and into contact with the flesh (to say nothing of the fist) of others. Meanwhile, we have no description here of Stephen, but only a synecdoche: his hair in disarray, a condition most of us share when we get up from bed but from which Mulligan is exempt. For the rest, in stark contrast to the detailed and suggestive portrait of Mulligan, we have a sense of Stephen as disembodied, clothed in the cast-offs of an unknown or, worse, in the boots of a Buck, treating his flesh as a confession box for the spirit.

In "Proteus," after experimenting with the "ineluctable modality of the audible," Stephen opens his eyes to see a bitter travesty of birth amidst desolation in the Irish wasteland. His response is a flood of imagery richer even than the reality apprehended by Bloom but deriving from his hoard of knowledge-nuts imaginatively reconstituted:

> They came down the steps from Leahy's terrace prudently, *Frauenzimmer:* and down the shelving shore flabbily their splayed feet sinking in the silted sand. Like me, like Algy, coming down to our mighty mother. Number one swung lourdily her midwife's bag, the other's gamp poked in the beach. From the liberties, out for the day. Mrs. Florence MacCabe, relict of the late Patk MacCabe, deeply lamented, of Bride Street. One of her sisterhood lugged me squealing into life. Creation from nothing. What has she in the bag? A misbirth with a trailing navelcord, hushed in ruddy wool. The cords of all link back, strandentwining cable of all flesh. That is why mystic monks. Will you be as gods? Gaze in your omphalos. Hello. Kinch here. Put me on to Edenville. Aleph, alpha: nought, nought, one. (37–38)

While the playful narrator imposes poetic effects on prosy circumstance, Stephen speaks a sort of poetry in hard nuggets of prose. The contrast is deliberate and effective. We are aware that the first and third sentences record Stephen's impressions, while the rest deal with his reactions. The weak rhymes ("prudently" and "flabbily" echoed and reenforced by the contrived "lourdily"), the alliteration verging on onomatopoeia which follows a deliberately undistinguished opening, and the ambiguous reference in "flabbily" capture the movement and the appearance of the two sleazy midwives. To suggest sterility and closed options, the narrator joins with a comma two absurdly complementary ideas. One midwife, playing the feminine role with masculine vigor, carries the heavy bag, an insufficient womb, complete with inadequate babe. The other carries the male implement, an umbrella which she pokes into the barren sand. The image is all the more effective in the light of its analogue from the "Parable of the Plums," in which these same "Dublin vestals" project plum pits from the top of the Nelson pillar in another mock-fertility rite. Significantly, Stephen's first reaction is to begin composing the parable, starting as he does in "Aeolus" and later in "Scylla" with "local colour". (188) This should be followed, in accordance with his good Jesuit training, by "composition of place" but instead it leads him into a meditation on origins. Quickly abandoning his composition, Stephen asks "What has she in the bag?" Then, in the spirit of his dogsbody reference in "Telemachus," he identifies with the "misbirth," [12] which he brings into misbegotten life and imaginatively returns to the womb for a telephone conversation with the primal mother who, as we soon learn, should have no navel. Further, through the mystic telephone number ("Aleph, alpha: nought, nought, one"), he suggests that he too is a terminus, the omega or zero to Adam's alpha or one, thus predicting the apocalypse and casting himself in the role of Christ. Here too is the theosophical response to the problem of history and identity and Stephen's mockery of it, mockery that is not devoid of disappointment at another failed solution. The question Stephen wishes to ask of the lady in Edenville (both Eden and Edenborough) is perhaps the same he tries to ask his mother in "Circe." Through the medium of this paragraph, despite the jangle of moods, modes, voices, and attitudes, Joyce effectively takes us from a simple realistic statement to the breakdown of communication into letters, numbers, and mystic symbols for the ineffable, which Stephen so bitterly mocks.

Stephen is much less his own man than he would like to be. Not only does he lean on his training (turning it of course to new ends), but also, as the interpolated second sentence shows, he returns automatically even in the privacy of his thoughts to Mulligan, whose words and behavior dominate his day almost as much as Molly's words and behavior dominate Bloom's, but to opposite effect. Stephen's play with Mulligan's Swinburne is especially significant in view of Buck's attempt to relate his Jesuit training to his failure as a poet: "They drove his wits astray . . . by visions of hell," Buck tells Haines in "Wandering Rocks." "He will never capture the Attic note. The note of Swinburne, of all poets, the white death and the ruddy birth. That is his tragedy. He can never be a poet." (249)[13] Here, in this most solipsistic of passages which speaks of urgent concerns, Buck speaks through the image of the "misbirth . . . hushed in ruddy wool," through the nickname Kinch, through the omphalos reference and probably even through the playful device of the spirit telephone call.

V

Given the quality of his mind and predilections, we may expect Bloom's mental stream to be far less dense in ideas and allusions than Stephen's. Still, we find in a characteristic passage a remarkable density and luminosity of effects and similar though perhaps less startling juxtapositions. Here for example is a bit from Bloom's frustrating conversation with M'Coy in "Lotus Eaters":

—I was with Bob Doran, he's on one of his periodical bends, and what do you call him Bantam Lyons. Just down there in Conway's we were.

Doran, Lyons in Conway's. She raised a gloved hand to her hair.

> In came Hoppy. Having a wet. Drawing back his head and gazing
> far from beneath his veiled eyelids he saw the bright fawn skin shine
> in the glare, the braided drums. Clearly I can see today. Moisture
> about gives long sight perhaps. Talking of one thing or another. Lady's
> hand. Which side will she get up? (74)

Three actions are made simultaneous in this passage: the narration
of the meeting with Hoppy Holohan (a Dublin character who plays
a minor but amusing part in the story "A Mother"), M'Coy's conversation through which the tale impinges on Bloom's consciousness,
and the gently erotic vision of the "haughty" lady adjusting her
gloves across the street. Add to this Bloom's sense of himself and
his modest experiment with the light ("Clearly I can see today."). It
is in the spirit of this chapter that the levels, though disparate, do
not clash dramatically. We may however smile at the juxtaposition
of Bloom's lust and his scientific interest while he is listening to the
small talk of a cadger angling for the loan of a piece of luggage. As
usual, the subtler verbal effects are in the narrator's voice. Bloom's
reflections on the lady are no match for what we know he sees. Paradoxically, what he sees is erotic only in its expression which must
correspond to his apprehension. Joyce is doing in his second sentence precisely the sort of thing he has done in the *Portrait* (see the
bird-girl of chapter 4), where a minimal gesture is invested with
hidden power. The prospect of the "bright fawn skin" suggests
brighter prospects, while the military and masterful tone of "braided
drums" goes beyond the object described, giving an early instance of
Bloom's masochism. The gesture, whose grace we must imagine, fills
us, like Bloom, with mute anticipation. Playing with Bloom, teasing
us, withholding the proffered rewards, however slight they may be,
the narrator is at his best when, a few lines after our paragraph, he
mentions, "High brown boots with laces dangling," and then has
Bloom reflect, "Proud: rich: silk stockings." Saying nothing, exposing nothing, he has suggested an object worthy of our expectant
gaze and prepared us humorously to be comically let down by the
carefully isolated couplet which culminates the passage:

> Watch! Watch! Silk flash rich stockings white. Watch!
> A heavy tramcar honking its gong slewed between. (74)

Every item in our paragraph will reappear elsewhere as will the
emotional climate. The sensual moment is fulfilled in "Nausikaa"
and travestied in "Circe." The conversation with M'Coy is increased
a thousandfold in "Cyclops," where the incident he recites is given
an amusing twist by Bob Doran, deeper than ever in his cups, who
explodes into incredulous surprise on hearing the news for the

second time (302–303). Bloom's experiment foreshadows his self-exploration in the second half of "Nausikaa." His thirsty but innocent gaze is more than matched by Stephen's guilty mocking memory in "Proteus," "You prayed to the devil in Serpentine avenue that the fubsy widow in front might lift her clothes still more from the wet street." (40) Ultimately each of these and other echoes must be taken into consideration as qualities latent in this passage.

Bloom's stream of consciousness is always readily identifiable. Despite the arranger's manipulation of his thought and the shifts in tone and emphasis, it retains throughout a vigor at once naïve and inventive that reflects on his native intelligence and maintains our respect even in his darkest hour. In the following paragraph of unmediated thought, Bloom, who has just left the Ormond bar, is walking to the music of a band:

> Instruments. A blade of grass, shell of her hands, then blow. Even comb and tissuepaper you can knock a tune out of. Molly in her shift in Lombard street west, hair down. I suppose each kind of trade made its own, don't you see? Hunter with a horn. Haw. Have you the? *Cloche. Sonnez la!* Shepherd his pipe. Policeman a whistle. Locks and keys! Sweep! Four o'clock's all's well! Sleep! All is lost now. Drum? Pompedy. Wait, I know. Towncrier, bumbailiff. Long John. Waken the dead. Pom. Dignam. Poor little *nominedomine*. Pom. It is music, I mean of course it's all pom pom pom very much what they call *da capo*. Still you can hear. As we march we march along, march along. Pom. (289)

Here the musical references provide most of the substance and even dictate the tempo, but the randomness, the spirit of inquiry, the rhetorical level is unmistakably Bloomish. It is past four and Boylan has reached Molly, the ultimate siren in this chapter full of mantraps. Ulysses-Bloom, drawn to her but paralysed by fear and guilt, resists her charms when he decides through indecision not to follow Boylan. Joyce insists on Molly's siren nature in the first part of the paragraph when he has Bloom view her hand as a shell and associate the comb with her long hair. In the previous paragraph, Bloom and the blind stripling (Stephen's surrogate) have sailed past the portrait of a cigarette-ad siren with her "hair all streaming" and earlier the barmaids behind their reef of counter have listened to a shell. But the allusion is important mainly as a symptom of Bloom's mental anguish as repeatedly he tries to turn his thoughts away from 7 Eccles Street and repeatedly he fails. The appropriateness of the musical comb to woman combined with the vision of Molly in her shift during happier times lead him to begin working out the origins of musical instruments, or rather to begin a forced inner conversation complete with a nervous "don't you see." Unfortunately, the hunter's horn, his first example of an instrument made by members of a trade, has sexual implications and worse. Hunter is the name of a watch which reminds him of the time of Boylan's appointment and, by virtue of his misunderstanding of the French *"cloche"* (bell), of the erotic play which helped Boylan prepare himself to pursue his quarry. Bloom quickly shifts to the shepherd's pipe which brings to mind the policeman and by extension the fact that he is at this moment being robbed. Locks and keys refer not only to protection but also to the lack of protection.[14] Not only is Bloom keyless, but, as we read in "Nausikaa," "Love laughs at locksmiths" (364); given the nature of his marriage, his key would offer slight protection. Perhaps thinking of another way to enter a house, he turns again to his obsession; for the sweep (whose only instrument is a phallic broom) calls to mind the rhyme "sleep" and once more the time of Boylan's appointment, disguised as a towncrier's "Four o'clock's all's well!" Apparently, there is no escape through logic and in fact "All is lost now." [15] So he turns quickly and in desperation to the sounds around him, the sounds of the band that pulls him into marching step, dragging his thoughts into its catchy rhythmical nothought, free at last. In this paragraph as in many others the thought serves as a screen through which meanings are perceived. At the same time it helps convey the man in the fullness of his experience with poignant immediacy and illustrates one of the functions of his feverish associations, namely, to mask his anxiety, guilt feelings, and insecurity not from the world but from himself. It is worth noting how well stocked his mind is with objects and objective associations and how cleverly he can relate those items which are not derived from automatic associations. It is also characteristic of him that his thought is too weak to resist intrusions, but strong enough to carry him through a number of barriers. Thus he does not abandon the thread of trades until the emotional pressure and the insistent rhythm render thought impossible.

The kaleidoscopic treatment of events in "Circe" may be seen as one sort of extension for the multiplication of objects and obsessions in Bloom's stream of consciousness. Another sort is available in the following excerpt from "Eumaeus" in which Bloom's immediate subject is the talkative sailor, whose lies give this chapter its homeric flavor:

> However, reverting to friend Sinbad and his horrifying adventures (who reminded him a bit of Ludwig, *alias* Ledwidge, when he occupied the boards of the Gaiety when Michael Gunn was identified with the management in the *Flying Dutchman*, a stupendous success, and his

host of admirers came in large numbers, everyone simply flocking to
hear him though ships of any sort, phantom or the reverse, on the
stage usually fell a bit flat as also did trains), there was nothing in-
trinsically incompatible about it, he conceded. On the contrary, that
stab in the back touch was quite in keeping with those Italianos,
though candidly he was none the less free to admit those ice creamers
and friers in the fish way, not to mention the chip potato variety and
so forth, over in little Italy there, near the Coombe, were sober thrifty
hardworking fellows except perhaps a bit too given to pothunting the
harmless necessary animal of the feline persuasion . . . (636–37)

Held by our expectation that something significant will take place
when the two wanderers are joined, rewarded by the scraps of action
that filter through, we are teased and diverted by a rhetoric which
might belong to the Bloomish author of a prize titbit. As some of
Samuel Beckett's voices have shown us, there is esthetic and metaphysical merit in saying so little and suggesting so much. We hang on
through the irrelevant parentheses, the journalistic circumlocutions,
the needless qualifications, the nonsequitors, the mixed metaphors,
the senseless affectations, the malapropisms, the redundancies, indeed through a catalogue of rhetorical sins that vies for completeness with the battery of rhetorical devices used in "Aeolus" to support the windy metaphor. All the while we know that Bloom, who
has no real point to make, is fooling himself more than Stephen,
who could not care less. Our most immediate rewards are the verbal
accidents (as numerous as the objects and events that animate
Bloom's monologues) which have usurped the role of action and experience and which absorb us as would some fantastic conjuring
trick. Will the narrator be able to find a new obstacle to expression,
a new source of embarrassment to flaunt our need to sustain Bloom
in the presence of his young judge? Just when we know he must
have finished, we find that he has another rabbit, and another. In
our comic desperation we grab for the first solid fact that comes our
way, even the hilarious description of the only Italians Bloom has
seen, "those ice creamers and friers in the fish way, not to mention
the chip potato variety and so forth, over in little Italy there, near
the Coombe." Reading such a passage is like grasping a bubble or a
spirit, or the essence of the divine, but then we may wonder what
God the Father had to say to his only son in paradise. Having sub-
sumed everything through his experience, Bloom, like God, knows
nothing.

The narrative strategy here makes us accomplices in unveiling
the one who reveals. At the same time it mutes and mimes the
drama of the encounter. Paradoxically, we are being served up

Bloom's stream of consciousness grotesquely distorted and diluted as narrative or rather as a narrative account of a conversation. We are as usual aware of the sources of Bloom's ideas, and we may also sense that the same process that led to Stephen's brilliant compositions here leads to dull-thudding and hilarious banality. Still, though the narrator is probably accurate about the content, Bloom could never be this humorless and pedestrian in his expression. The least sympathetic of his commentators is kinder to him than this literary projection. Faced with an unfriendly witness like the narrator of "Cyclops," we are willing to discount even the truth and sympathize with a well-meaning bumbler in a tight spot. Faced with a friendly but inept one, we are forced to laugh twice through our sympathy and admit even in the absence of other evidence that the little dun is right: "if you said to Bloom: *Look at, Bloom. Do you see that straw? That's a straw.* Declare to my aunt he'd talk about it for an hour so he would and talk steady." (316)

Like Ulysses at the swineherd's, the usually forthright traveler can be astonishingly devious, but unlike his model, he is a poor dissembler. It is not so much his transparent motives as what he unconsciously says that enthralls us. The references to such travelers as Sinbad and the Flying Dutchman recall the Wandering Jew and Ulysses and the unquiet ghosts that haunt both men. The *"alias"* which does not conceal, suggests the disguises of Ulysses but conveys the inadequate masks of Bloom himself and underlines his pathetic ineptness at this moment. The pantomime at the Gaiety continues a motif introduced through Stephen's musings in "Telemachus" (10). Here it adds the dimension of sentimental farce and points back to "Circe." When Bloom mentions that Ludwig's "host of admirers came in large numbers," we may recall his slip in "Cyclops" ("the wife's admirers" (313)) and discover another even more Freudian slip in the play on ejaculation. The remainder of the paragraph contains a slur on the Italians which, though gentle and, like all of Bloom's expressions of sentiment, well-meant, echoes anti-Semitic clichés. Bloom's real point, concealed by an inept subterfuge, is that passion is exciting and his Mediterranean Molly is passionate; his real need is to share her with Stephen, make himself interesting through her glamour, air his obsession, and express obliquely his distress over her adultery. Ironically, he is exposing himself as a naïve and home-loving romantic to the guilty romantic who has earlier glamourized the wanderer in the Jew.

It is tempting to round out this discussion of Joyce's effects as they relate to meaning by treating briefly his handling of one of the book's minor cruxes, the infidelity of Molly as attested to by the list of twenty-five lovers (not suitors) in "Ithaca." For all its apparent objectivity, the list, like other items in this chapter, is a delightful fraud or at least an equivocation. We read: "Assuming Mulvey to be the first term of his series, Penrose, Bartell d'Arcy, professor Goodwin, Julius Mastiansky, John Henry Menton, Father Bernard Corrigan . . . Hugh E. (Blazes) Boylan and so each and so on to nolast term." (731) Though most readers fail to notice, this is "his," that is, Bloom's account and hence of doubtful value if not simply a projection of his masochistic fancy. The narrator has done little more than arrange the "lovers" chronologically. No wonder some of the individual items are absurd and Lieutenant Gardner, one of Molly's most ardent suitors (749), is omitted. Still we fall readily into the trap prepared for us by the arranger who, playing on our prior hearsay knowledge, permits us to turn the neophyte adulteress into a whore. In this way the naturalistic texture is both subverted and maintained and Molly's symbolic eminence established. The joke on us is a serious one, a function of the style and a reflection of a possible reality. Molly *could be* a great whore and the *Magna Mater,* but she *is* a lazy, ignorant bundle of instincts tied to middle class values, though endowed with a fairly good singing voice, a hot temper, a sense of humor, and ample dimensions. If the superobjective voice of "Ithaca" fails to tell us this, the subjective effusion of "Penelope" reveals all, giving the lie to the list and altering many of our preconceptions. One example will suffice to illustrate the efficacy of Joyce's methods:

> . . . I wish some man or other would take me sometime when hes there and kiss me in his arms theres nothing like a kiss long and hot down to your soul almost paralyses you then I hate that confession when I used to go to Father Corrigan he touched me father and what harm if he did where and I said on the canal bank like a fool but wereabouts on your person my child on the leg behind high up was it yes rather high up . . . I always think of the real father what did he want to know for when I already confessed it to God he had a nice fat hand the palm moist always I wouldn't [sic] mind feeling it neither would he Id say by the bullneck in his horsecollar . . . I could see his face he couldnt see mine of course hed never turn or let on still his eyes were red when his father died theyre lost for a woman of course must be terrible when a man cries let alone them Id like to be embraced by one in his vestments . . . (740–41)

We can scratch Father Bernard Corrigan from Bloom's list, or can we? Molly has enjoyed him in the abstract if not in the flesh and the Bible speaks of ocular lust. If Molly's desire turns out to be not much stronger than Bloom's voyeuristic impulses, her expression of desire ("a kiss long and hot down to your soul almost paralyses you") has the validity of Stephen's imaginings in "Proteus." (49) To our minds there is only a superficial difference between these vivid fantasies and the actions they describe. It is worth noting that Molly's yearning is more appropriate to an adolescent than to a hardened woman. Still, she has had no relations with a priest, and she will go on to disprove most of the list in detail and to show herself to be even less worldly than Bloom and almost as faithful as Penelope.

The most striking effect of Molly's utterance is the flow conveyed not only by the lack of punctuation but also by the tone and especially by the proliferation of pronouns. When, rather than complete the sentence beginning "when I used to go to Father Corrigan," Molly begins a new one with the ambiguous "he touched me," she provides the hint followed up later with her reflections on his "fat hand." In a parallel development Bloom is subtly identified with the priest through the title "father" which reminds Molly "of the real father" and generates the aside, "still [Poldy's] eyes were red when his father died." Molly's undirected thought has led her to make a statement that reflects not only on her husband's curious abstinence but also on her unconscious wish that he resume relations. It is the reader, encouraged by the fluid juxtaposition, who completes both the identification and the thought. The closer we inspect this or any passage from Molly's monologue the richer its implications become. We may point in passing to the priestly hands, so important in the *Portrait* as emblems of another sort of humanity, or to the confession, which is focal to Stephen's experience and foreign to Bloom's, or to the paternity theme, or to "paralysis" which characterizes the Dublin scene as well as the lives of Molly and Bloom, or to the bulls and horses seen among other things as sacrificial animals and fertility symbols. Each of them is touched lightly here. Like her reputation, Molly's monologue can carry or dissolve anything. It is the ideal response both to male objectivity and to the crystalline profusion of "Circe" since it naturalizes excess through verbal illusion. Recalling the sort of magic that joins Stephen to Buck in "Telemachus," we see that in this sense too Joyce has come full circle, elaborating a style whose very simplicity and directness can prove endlessly evocative.

ཚོ CONCLUSION ༄

If, as experience shows, even the most straightforward plot summary will contain errors, the critical study, because it defends a
position, is bound to limit if not distort its object. It follows that
no book on *Ulysses* will do justice to it. Still, we can learn from
even the clumsiest effort, and this brief attempt to number the
book's qualities may give the reader a sense of it as complex and
coherent, austere and comic, difficult and accessible, capable of stirring us in many ways but always in terms of itself. If the reality
we perceive there is a mirror of the everyday in terms of the singular,
the singular thus perceived is increasingly familiar and dynamic and
very like our own singularity. The object of our contemplation and
our experience of it are increasingly one. But it is not in terms of
the end result that we should think of this book but rather of the
process of apprehension. Our movement through it is its own reward
and virtually endless, for the object will never be fully perceived.
Ulysses can be seen as a collection of skillfully arranged vibrations
whose intensity will depend on our awareness of them and whose
number is variable. The source of these vibrations is the tension set
up among the qualities which I have tried to describe (and others
beyond the scope of so short a study). It follows that we cannot define *Ulysses* in terms of any one aspect though we may give precedence to its narrative and dramatic content. Further, in a work that
uses the moment to suggest eternity and the geographical point to
suggest infinity, there can be no more question of moral positions
than there can be of conclusions.

Finally, there is the question of judgment. There are certainly
flaws in the fabric of *Ulysses*, imbalance, overingenious symbolism,
dead spaces filled by the author's wit, but the ultimate criteria in
this case should be the book's vitality and the seemingly inexhaust-
ible interest it generates in generations of readers. And besides, who
can sort out flaws in the three-ring circus where in the turbulence of
the endless moment each individual flaw resists detection or pales to
insignificance? The negative criticism of *Ulysses* that most affected

101

Joyce during his lifetime was in Wyndham Lewis' *Time and Western Man* which among other things attacked Joyce as a follower of Bergson and Einstein and labeled Bloom a stage Jew standing in for Joyce himself. Joyce responded obliquely, as was his wont, but at length in *Finnegans Wake*. To Frank Budgen he said, "Allowing that the whole of what Lewis says about my book is true, is it more than ten percent of the truth?"

JOYCE'S SCHEMA

AUTHOR'S NOTE: I have corrected obvious spelling errors and regularized Joyce's punctuation while maintaining his spelling of proper names even when it is at variance with my own.

Title	Scene	Hour	Organ	Art
I TELEMACHIA				
1 Telemachus	The Tower	8 a.m.		theology
2 Nestor	The School	10 a.m.		history
3 Proteus	The Strand	11 a.m.		philology
II ODYSSEY				
1 Calypso	The House	8 a.m.	kidney	economics
2 Lotuseaters	The Bath	10 a.m.	genitals	botany, chemistry
3 Hades	The Graveyard	11 a.m.	heart	religion
4 Eolus	The Newspaper	12 noon	lungs	rhetoric
5 Lestrygonians	The Lunch	1 p.m.	esophagus	architecture
6 Scylla and Charybdis	The Library	2 p.m.	brain	literature
7 Wandering Rocks	The Streets	3 p.m.	blood	mechanics
8 Sirens	The Concert Room	4 p.m.	ear	music
9 Cyclops	The Tavern	5 p.m.	muscle	politics
10 Nausikaa	The Rocks	8 p.m.	eye, nose	painting
11 Oxen of Sun	The Hospital	10 p.m.	womb	medicine
12 Circe	The Brothel	12 midnight	locomotor apparatus	magic
III NOSTOS				
1 Eumeus	The Shelter	1 a.m.	nerves	navigation
2 Ithaca	The House	2 a.m.	skeleton	science
3 Penelope	The Bed		flesh	

Colour	Symbol	Technic	Correspondences
white gold	heir	narrative (young)	(Stephen – Telemachus, Hamlet : Buck Mulligan – Antinous : Milkwoman – Mentor)
brown	horse	catechism (personal)	(Deasy – Nestor : Pisistratus – Sargent : Helen – Mrs O'Shea)
green	tide	monologue (male)	(Proteus – Primal Matter : Kevin Egan – Menelaus : Megapenthus – The Cocklepicker)
orange	nymph	narrative (mature)	(Calypso – The Nymph : Dlugacz – The Recall : Zion – Ithaca)
	eucharist	narcissism	(Lotuseaters – Cabhorses, Communicants, Soldiers, Eunuchs, Bather, Watchers of Cricket)
white black	caretaker	incubism	(Dodder, Grand and Royal Canals, Liffey – The 4 Rivers : Cunningham – Sisyphus : Father Coffey – Cerberus : Caretaker – Hades : Daniel O'Connell – Hercules : Dignam – Elpenor : Parnell – Agamemnon : Menton – Ajax)
red	editor	enthymemic	(Crawford – Eolus : Incest – Journalism : Floating Island – Press)
	constables	peristalsis	(Antiphates – Hunger : The Decoy – Food : Lestrygonians – Teeth)
	Stratford, London	dialectic	(The Rock – Aristotle, Dogma – Stratford : The Whirlpool – Plato, Mysticism, London : Ulysses – Socrates, Jesus, Shakespeare)
	citizens	labyrinth	(Bosphorus – Liffey : European bank – Viceroy : Asiatic bank – Conmee : Symplegades – Groups of Citizens)
	barmaids	fuga per canonem	(Sirens – Barmaids : Isle – Bar)
	fenian	gigantism	(Noman – I : Stake – Cigar : Challenge – Apotheosis)
grey, blue	virgin	tumescence detumescence	(Phaeacia – Star of the Sea : Gerty – Nausikaa)
white	mothers	embryonic development	(Hospital – Trinacria : Lampetie, Phaethusa – Nurses : Helios – Horne : Oxen – Fertility : Crime – Fraud)
	whore	hallucination	(Circe – Bella)
	sailors	narrative (old)	(Eumeus – Skin the Goat : Sailor – Ulysses Pseudangelos : Melanthius – Corley)
	comets	catechism (impersonal)	(Eurymachus – Boylan : Suitors – Scruples : Bow – Reason)
	earth	monologue (female)	(Penelope – Earth : Web – Movement)

≈§ APPENDIX II §≈

CHRONOLOGY

1882   Birth of James Aloysius Joyce in Dublin on February 2.
On May 6 the Invincibles commit the Phoenix Park murders in Dublin.

1888–91   Joyce attends Clongowes Wood School.
Parnell's trials and death (1890–91).
Symbolism blooms in France (1886–98).

1893–98   Joyce attends Belvedere College.
Trials of Oscar Wilde (1896).
Rise and fall of aestheticism.

1898–1902 Joyce attends University College.
W. B. Yeats's *The Countess Cathleen* becomes a storm center for the Irish literary theatre (1899).
The Dreyfus affair rocks France (Zola's *J'accuse,* 1898).
Sigmund Freud formulates his major psychoanalytic theories.

1902–4   Paris and return. Death of his mother (August 13, 1903). Departure with Nora Barnacle into exile: Pola, Trieste.
Yeats, Moore, Lady Gregory and AE active in the Irish literary renaissance.
Edward VII succeeds Victoria.
Russo-Japanese War (1904).

1909–12   Two trips to Dublin: to found a cinema, and push the publication of *Dubliners.*
The period of German expressionism and of Picasso's and Braque's experiments with cubism.

1914   Publication of *Dubliners* by Grant Richards in London. Serial publication of *A Portrait of the Artist as a Young Man* begins in *The Egoist.*
World War I.

1915   Move to Zurich.
Easter rebellion in Dublin.
Einstein announces his general theory of relativity (1913–16).

1916–17   Publication of *A Portrait of the Artist as a Young Man* by B. W. Huebsch in New York.
Start of the Russian Revolution on October 25, 1917.

1918   Publication of *Exiles* by Grant Richards in London. Serial publication of *Ulysses* begins in *The Little Review*. Harriet Weaver becomes his Maecenas.
World War I ends on November 11.

1920   Joyce moves with his family from Paris to Trieste.
The Government of Ireland Act establishes separate parliaments for North and South (rejected by the South).

1922   *The Little Review* is prosecuted in America for the publication of parts of *Ulysses*. Publication of *Ulysses* by Sylvia Beach in Paris.
The Irish Free State is proclaimed.

1927   Serial publication of *Finnegans Wake* begins in *transition*.
Joyce is the silent center of a new movement in Paris.
Surrealism flourishes in France.

1933   The lifting of the ban permits publication of *Ulysses* in America.
Hitler named Reichschancellor on January 30.

1939   Publication of *Finnegans Wake* by Faber and Faber in London and Viking Press in New York.
World War II begins after invasion of Poland on September 1.

1941   Death in Zurich on January 13.

✌ NOTES ✍

Chapter I

1. *Ulysses* (New York: Random House, 1961). All page references in the text are to this edition. No current edition of *Ulysses* is completely reliable, but the errors are not apt to distract the general reader.

2. *Finnegans Wake* (New York: Viking Press, 1939), p. 288.

3. Richard Ellmann, *James Joyce* (New York: Oxford University Press, 1965), p. 10.

4. See *A Portrait of the Artist as a Young Man* (New York: Viking Press, 1964), p. 165.

5. For a balanced discussion of Joyce's training see Kevin Sullivan, *Joyce Among the Jesuits* (New York: Columbia University Press, 1958).

6. For earlier versions and a succinct discussion see Richard Ellmann and Ellsworth Mason, eds., James Joyce, *The Critical Writings* (New York: Viking Press, 1959), pp. 141–48 and *passim*.

7. Ellmann, *James Joyce*, p. 178. The number of years was reduced in *Ulysses* (p. 249) to coincide with the gestation period of the *Portrait*: "Dublin 1904, Trieste 1914."

8. Ellmann, *James Joyce*, pp. 238–39.

9. *Finnegans Wake*, p. 112.

10. See the decision of the United States District Court included in *Ulysses*, pp. vii–xii.

11. See "The Day of the Rabblement" in *The Critical Writings*, pp. 68–72.

12. Ellmann, *James Joyce*, p. 51.

13. Robert Scholes and Richard M. Kain, eds., *The Workshop of Daedalus, James Joyce and the Raw Materials for A Portrait of the Artist as a Young Man* (Evanston, Ill.: Northwestern University Press, 1965), pp. 11–51. Reprinted in *A Portrait of the Artist as a Young Man*, ed. Chester Anderson (New York: Viking Press, 1968), pp. 257–266.

14. Ellmann, *James Joyce*, p. 169.

15. Scholes, *The Workshop of Daedalus*, p. 60.

16. *The Critical Writings*, p. 71.

17. Scholes, *The Workshop of Daedalus*, p. 60. His actual words are important: ". . . a portrait is not an identificative paper but rather the curve of an emotion." This idea, derived probably from the French literary historian Hippolyte

108

Taine, implies a steady development along determined lines, a development resulting from a combination of nature and nurture and marked by choices freely made but determined by the bent and capacities of the individual.

Chapter II

1. This position contradicts the accepted view that Molly is an experienced and hardened adultress, a view which renders Bloom's distress incomprehensible, undercuts the significance of Molly's monologue and weakens the coherence and narrative structure of *Ulysses*. However, independently of each other, Robert Martin Adams (*Ulysses: Surface and Symbol,* New York: Oxford, 1962; pp. 35–43) and Stanley Sultan (*The Argument of Ulysses,* Columbus, Ohio: Ohio University Press, 1964; pp. 431–434) have demonstrated Molly's relative chastity.

2. It is characteristic of Joyce's irony that the tower built to keep the French out of Ireland houses the dilettante Mulligan and the Francophile Stephen.

3. *Portrait,* p. 172.

4. Frank Budgen, *James Joyce and the Making of Ulysses,* rev. ed., (Bloomington, Ind.: Indiana University Press, 1960), p. 45.

5. In "Nestor," when Deasy says, "You have two copies there. If you can have them published at once," Stephen automatically thinks, "*Telegraph, Irish Homestead.*" (*Ulysses,* p. 35)

6. When the funeral procession passes Boylan during "Hades," Bloom covers his embarrassment in a similar way: "Mr Bloom reviewed the nails of his left hand, then those of his right hand." (*Ulysses,* p. 92)

7. For a comprehensive discussion of Joyce's method and sources, see William M. Schutte, *Joyce and Shakespeare: A Study in the Meaning of "Ulysses"* (New Haven: Yale University Press, 1957).

8. There is an unmistakable echo here of the Marquess of Queensbury, the brutal father of Oscar Wilde's lover, Lord Alfred Douglas, and the cause of Wilde's perdition. Joyce has ironically altered this suggestive circumstance, as he has all others.

9. The timing of this event at 11:10 p.m. suggests the time of the broken appointment at The Ship, 11:30 a.m. Joyce is playing on Telemachus' escape from the suitors waiting in ambush for him after his trip (see also Hamlet's treatment of Rosencrantz and Guildenstern). The circumstances are reversed, or so it seems. The suitors escape and not Telemachus, but the account we get is vague enough to allow for the play of fancy.

10. For a full account of their addresses and his jobs see Molly's monologue. (*Ulysses,* p. 772)

11. Bloom's Masonic connections, which function as a parallel for Athena's protection of Ulysses, also help explain the edge he seems to have on the other Jews in the book.

12. The reference is to Dan Dawson's speech, which gets short shrift even from the journalists.

13. Implicit in this image is the view that it would take a combination of two natures to make a Shakespeare for our times. But since we move quickly from an identity of opposites to a father-son relationship, it is worth noting the role played by Shakespeare in the view of Stephen as Bloom's spiritual son. By a sort of metempsychosis ("O, rocks! . . . Tell us in plain words," Molly-Calypso says.

(64)), Joyce links Shakespeare who lost an eleven-year-old son Hamnet, to Bloom whose son, dead at eleven days, would now be almost eleven, to Stephen who is now twenty-two but who met Bloom eleven years ago.

Chapter III

1. Arnold Goldman, *The Joyce Paradox: Form and Freedom in His Fiction* (Evanston, Ill.: Northwestern University Press, 1966). Though I would question Joyce's use of Kierkegaard as a source, this view is helpful in distinguishing between Stephen's and Bloom's modes.

2. See especially Adams, *Ulysses: Surface and Symbol*.

3. The first of these was taken by Joyce from his collection of epiphanies (see Scholes and Kain, *Workshop of Daedalus*, p. 31) and carefully altered to fit the circumstance. See the reference to "harpy" and "bloodless" and the dumbshow effect.

4. Amusingly, after Joyce's death, the original for this original, Dr. Oliver St. John Gogarty, accused Joyce, his recreator, of perpetrating a hoax on the world when he wrote *Ulysses*, and called Joyce an "artist" in just this sense.

5. Here he is faithful to his model, who was thought to resemble his fellow Oxonian as an Irish wit and promising poet, and who like Wilde was "stately, plump."

6. In *Finnegans Wake*, the mocker, Shaun the post, says of his artist twin that he has written the darkness out of himself into a universal book very much like the one we would expect Stephen to write (and those Joyce wrote): ". . . and the first till last alshemist wrote over every square inch of the only foolscap available, his own body, till by its corrosive sublimation one continuous present tense integument slowly unfolded all marryvoising moodmoulded cyclewheeling history . . . but with each word that would not pass away the squidself which he had squirtscreened from the crystalline world waned chagreenold and doriangrayer in its dudhud." (*Finnegans Wake*, pp. 185–86)

7. *Portrait*, p. 247.

Chapter IV

1. Budgen, *James Joyce*, pp. 16–17.

2. *Ibid.*, p. 20.

3. Joyce's list of "Correspondences" is incomplete. His Proteus, for example, is "Primal Matter" while his Menelaus is Kevin Egan. No mention is made of Uncle Richie, who is Menelaus as host, or Stephen, who is Menelaus fighting protean flux. See Appendix I.

4. Stuart Gilbert, *James Joyce's "Ulysses"* (New York: Random House, Inc., Vintage Books, 1955), pp. 65–76.

5. For a discussion of this and other aspects of the Shakespeare parallel see Schutte, *Joyce and Shakespeare*, pp. 18–20 and *passim*.

6. "Is he an old man or a young man? Where are his home and family? . . . And he can't be complete because he's never alone." (Budgen, *James Joyce*, p. 16)

7. Ellmann, *James Joyce*, p. 275.

8. This image is consistent with a statement he makes to himself in "Scylla" where, a doctor among the doct, he reacts to a Wagner-like Mr Best: "Wit. You would give your five wits for youth's proud livery he pranks in." (*Ulysses*, p. 199)

9. Gilbert, *James Joyce's "Ulysses,"* p. 320–23.

10. For a review of these positions and their application see William York Tindall, *James Joyce: His Way of Interpreting the Modern World* (New York: Charles Scribner's Sons, 1950). See also Samuel Beckett's perceptive article, "Dante . . . Bruno. Vico . . . Joyce" in Samuel Beckett, *et al., Our Exagmination Round his Factification for Incamination of "Work in Progress"* (Norfolk, Va.: New Directions, 1939). What these writers have to say about Bruno and *Finnegans Wake* can in some measure be applied to *Ulysses.*

11. The immediate reference is to Paddy Dignam, dying and dead.

12. "Jewgreek is greekjew. Extremes meet. Death is the highest form of life. Bah!" *(Ulysses,* p. 504) This is an obvious reference to Stephen's meeting with Bloom and their opposite identity but it also refers to the Judeo-Hellenic nature of our heritage and doubtless to one of Stephen's theories. Typically, the source of the remark is ambiguous. It is assigned to Lynch's cap, but it may be Stephen's hallucination, a mode of self-criticism.

13. *Ulysses,* p. 213.

14. Richard Ellmann *(James Joyce,* p. 351) notes the similarity between this statement and Croce's précis of the work of another of Joyce's favorite philosophers, Giambattista Vico's *The New Science.* Apparently Stephen is moving from one predilection to another in his ceaseless effort to define his predicament.

15. Goldman, *The Joyce Paradox,* p. 158.

16. Clive Hart, *James Joyce's "Ulysses"* (Sydney, Australia: Sydney University Press, 1968), p. 73.

17. A reference to the affair Milly has begun with Bannon.

18. Here both the affair now beginning with Boylan and the resumption of sex with Molly are alluded to.

19. See this in relation to Stephen's response to Deasy's appeal to justice before generosity: "I fear those big words . . . which make us so unhappy." *(Ulysses,* p. 31)

20. See also the stellar sign Stephen claims appeared at Shakespeare's birth *(Ulysses,* p. 210) and his image of the falling Lucifer *(Ibid.,* p. 50).

21. Hart, *James Joyce's "Ulysses,"* pp. 74–75.

Chapter V

1. S. L. Goldberg, *James Joyce* (New York: Grove Press, 1962), p. 95.

2. See Richard Ellmann, ed., *Letters of James Joyce* (New York: Viking Press, 1966), II, p. 409. For a discussion of the technique see Melvin J. Friedman, *Stream of Consciousness: a Study of Literary Method* (New Haven: Yale University Press, 1956), pp. 210–43, and Robert Humphrey, *Stream of Consciousness in the Modern Novel* (Berkeley: University of California Press, 1954), *passim.* Robert H. Demming gives two pages of further reading on the subject in *A Bibliography of James Joyce Studies* (Lawrence, Kansas: University of Kansas Libraries, 1964), pp. 110–11.

3. *Finnegans Wake,* p. 613.

4. Joyce took obvious pleasure in identifying the history of the Irish and the Jews, two conquered nations originating in opposite corners of the west and spreading out in opposite directions in exile and non-nationhood.

5. *Portrait*, p. 50.

6. In connection with these first six chapters, it is worth recalling Stephen and Joyce's theory of modes:

> The lyrical form is in fact the simplest verbal vesture of an instant of emotion. . . . He who utters it is more conscious of the instant of emotion than of himself as feeling emotion. The simplest epical form is seen emerging out of lyrical literature when the artist prolongs and broods upon himself as the centre of an epical event and this form progresses till the centre of emotional gravity is equidistant from the artist himself and from others. The narrative is no longer purely personal. The personality of the artist passes into the narration itself, flowing round and round the persons and the action. . . . The dramatic form is reached when the vitality which has flowed and eddied around each person fills every person with such vital force that he or she assumes a proper and intangible esthetic life. (*Portrait*, pp. 214–15)

Substituting the word character for the term "artist" we find that Stephen's chapters roughly approximate the movement from "dramatic" to "lyric" while Bloom's, operating in the comic rather than the serious or romantic mode, move from lyrical to dramatic in the proper order. Joyce appears to be checking out ironically his own theory.

7. Significantly, Stephen is called "Mocker" here, an identity generally reserved for Mulligan.

8. This strategy, together with an almost Dickensian treatment of character and incident was taken over by Virginia Woolf in her first experimental effort, *Mrs. Dalloway*, in which a pair of motifs unites people from all walks in various parts of Westminster at a given hour of the morning.

9. For further comment see Gilbert (*James Joyce's "Ulysses,"* pp. 294–312) as well as A. M. Klein's extremely elaborate analysis of the obstetrical metaphor in "Oxen of the Sun" (*Here and Now*, I, January 1949, pp. 28–48).

10. Constantine P. Curran, *James Joyce Remembered* (New York: Oxford University Press, 1968), p. 29.

11. The gross and powerful image of irremediable sterility that punctuates Bloom's vision does not preclude the appeal to the spiritual East or the validity of the life image, though, like the actual cloud that inspires it, it casts both in shadow.

12. In this connection see little Rudy in lambswool.

13. It is characteristic of Stephen that though he too uses Dryden's words ("Cousin Swift, you will never be a poet"), unlike Mulligan, he applies them with significant alteration to himself in a protean context: "Cousin Stephen, you will never be a saint." (*Ulysses*, p. 40)

14. See also the description of the key and lock as a male-female couple in "Ithaca," p. 703.

15. The fact that this refers to the aria *"Tutto è sciolto"* deepens and trivializes Bloom's meaning, underlining both his lack of originality and his inability to express his anguish. For further comment on Joyce's use of musical allusion in "Sirens," see Weldon Thornton, *Allusions in "Ulysses"* (Chapel Hill: University of North Carolina Press, 1968).

BIBLIOGRAPHY

The following brief list, designed for the beginning reader of *Ulysses*, is of necessity very selective. For further information on the Joyce canon see the standard work by J. J. Slocum and Herbert Cahoon, *A Bibliography of James Joyce, 1882–1941*. New Haven: Yale University Press, 1953. For a useful checklist of criticism through 1961 see R. H. Demming, *A Bibliography of James Joyce Studies*. Lawrence, Kansas: University of Kansas Libraries, 1964. Supplementary checklists are to be found in numbers of the *James Joyce Quarterly* and in the annual bibliography of *PMLA*. A good selected list has recently appeared in *Modern Fiction Studies* (Vol. XV, No. 1. Spring 1969), pp. 105–182.

PRIMARY SOURCES. The following works are not cited in the text.

Chamber Music, ed. William York Tindall. New York: Columbia University Press, 1954.

Dubliners, eds. Robert Scholes and A. Walton Litz. New York: Viking Press, 1969.

Exiles. New York: Viking Press, 1951. Contains Joyce's notes.

Giacomo Joyce, ed. Richard Ellmann. New York: Viking Press, 1968. A lyrical account of Joyce's passion for a young Triestine Jewess. This recently-discovered manuscript is interesting in the light of Stephen's and Bloom's romantic yearnings.

Letters of James Joyce, vol. I, ed. Stuart Gilbert. New York: Viking Press, 1957. Vols. II and III, ed. Richard Ellmann. New York: Viking Press, 1966. Of particular interest are the letters written prior to 1913, especially those addressed to Stanislaus and Nora Joyce.

Stephen Hero. New York: New Directions, 1963. Augmented text.

SECONDARY SOURCES. The following list does not include all of the items referred to in my footnotes.

Blamires, H., *The Bloomsday Book: A guide through Joyce's "Ulysses."* New York: Barnes & Noble, Inc., 1966. A page by page treatment of the action and some of the thematic substructure which, despite a number of misreadings and an undue emphasis on religious symbolism, is unusually reliable.

Budgen, Frank, *James Joyce and the Making of "Ulysses"* (rev. ed.). Bloomington, Ind.: Indiana University Press, 1960. Joyce's close friend and confidant during the Zurich years writes a lively, personal, critical account of the evolution and nature of *Ulysses*.

Curran, Constantine P., *James Joyce Remembered.* New York: Oxford University Press, 1968. The most literate of Joyce's university friends places him in the Dublin environment and exposes with great clarity his early influences.

Ellmann, Richard, *James Joyce.* New York: Oxford University Press, 1965. A critical biography that comes close to being definitive and supplants all previous works.

Gilbert, Stuart, *James Joyce's "Ulysses"* (rev. ed.). New York: Alfred A. Knopf, 1952. The earliest extended treatment, authorized by Joyce as a response to Wyndham Lewis's scathing but not unperceptive critique which accused Joyce of formlessness. Though he overemphasizes the intentions implied by Joyce's schema, Gilbert gives a good reading of the *Odyssey* parallel and an adequate if somewhat overstated treatment of certain symbols and themes.

Goldberg, S. L., *The Classical Temper: A Study of James Joyce's "Ulysses."* New York: Barnes & Noble, Inc., 1961. A coherent critical study of *Ulysses* as an "imaginative achievement" with significant chapters on the function of Stephen's esthetic theory in the *Portrait* and *Ulysses.*

Goldman, Arnold, *The Joyce Paradox: Form and Freedom in His Fiction.* Evanston, Ill.: Northwestern University Press, 1966. An attempt to reconcile opposing "symbolist" and "realist" views of Joyce's meaning, particularly those of Kenner and Goldberg. Goldman posits an unresolved tension between freedom and necessity in Joyce's work and the integration of character, theme, symbol and structure in *Ulysses.*

Hanley, Miles L., comp., *A Word-Index to James Joyce's "Ulysses"* (rev. ed.). Madison: University of Wisconsin Press, 1951. Though this index is keyed to the older Random House edition it remains a useful aid for readers wishing to trace references.

Hart, Clive, *James Joyce's "Ulysses."* Sydney, Australia: Sydney University Press, 1968. A concise and clear-headed discussion which includes a useful review of previous criticism.

Joyce, Stanislaus, *My Brother's Keeper.* Edited with an introduction and notes by Richard Ellmann, New York: Viking Press, 1958. The idiosyncratic but helpful memoirs of Joyce's early confidant.

Kenner, Hugh, *Dublin's Joyce.* Bloomington, Ind.: Indiana University Press, 1956. This book is best known for its somewhat overstated, but very necessary, view of Joyce's ironic stance. At a breakneck pace it also gives a rewarding commentary on many aspects of Joyce's work.

Murillo, L. A., *The Cyclical Night.* Cambridge: Harvard University Press, 1968. The best study to date of Joyce's use of irony (to achieve aesthetic stasis).

Sultan, Stanley, *The Argument of "Ulysses."* Columbus, Ohio: Ohio State University Press, 1964. Despite excessive length, an unfortunate moral bias, and occasional errors, this close reading contains many valuable insights.

Thornton, Weldon, *Allusions in "Ulysses."* Chapel Hill: University of North Carolina Press, 1968. A good guide through the jungle of literary, historical, and topical allusions in *Ulysses.*

Tindall, William York, *James Joyce: His Way of Interpreting the Modern World.* New York: Charles Scribner's Sons, 1950. A lively readable treatment of the Joyce canon as an integrated whole with special emphasis on the archetypal themes and prime sources.

INDEX

116